THE SEARCH FOR
THE PROMISED LAND

THE SEARCH FOR THE PROMISED LAND

A NEW/OLD CIVILIZATION PURSUES ITS GOAL

From Bible Times To Today, Seekers Who Were Changed By Encounters With The Largely-Unseen Spiritual Kingdom Became A Special Civilization Within Traditional Cultures—One Now Rising Rapidly And Prophesied To Overcome All Evil

by

Karl Roebling

Also By Karl Roebling

Is There Healing Power?
Not His Death, His Overcoming
    of Death
The Search For Jesus -The
    History and Future of Religion
Pentecostal Origins and Trends
    and others

FIRST EDITION

Copyright © 1998 Karl Roebling
All Rights Reserved

Printed in the United States of America

ISBN 0-942910-16-8

CONTENTS

PREFACE

God told Abraham to "get thee out...unto a land that I will shew thee." But was God directing the Patriarch to a material or spiritual land?

From Bible times to the present, seekers who encountered the spiritual kingdom in varying degrees found themselves changed, healed, protected, guided, supplied, strengthened, empowered.

These people have constituted a special civilization throughout Abraham's era, the later Exodus, and the still later centuries of Early Christianity. Largely blocked during the age of darkness, they pushed forward again in the reawakening and age of discovery.

Today, millions are seeking and partially finding the higher realm which is the true Promised Land. They are changing and rising while much of the West secularizes.

The Bible predicts struggle between forces of good ushering in the divine kingdom, and forces holding the world in evil's grip—but the prophesied "end" is only the end of evil (as in Rev. 21:4), by stages.

AUTHOR'S NOTE

The author believes the role of the individual in religion in the times ahead—much as in the early days of both Judaism and Christianity—must reappear on a very broad basis if the challenges prophesied in Scripture are to be met and overcome. Comments and experiences are invited at the address near the end.

**May My Little Friend
Find It**

THE SEARCH FOR
THE PROMISED LAND

1
THE TRAIL OF BLOOD FROM ABRAHAM TO AMERICA

"Get thee out...unto a land that I will shew thee," said God to Abram some 4,000 years ago. Thus began the long trek towards the Bible's "Promised Land"—a goal still not attained, in the eyes of many who continue to search.

With his wife Sarai and nephew Lot, Abram (later re-named Abraham) moved south from Haran into the "land of Canaan," where the "Lord appeared unto Abram, and said, Unto thy seed will I give this land" (see Gen. 11 and 12.)

After visiting Egypt and returning, Lot and Abram divided their herds. Lot chose the well-watered plain of Jordan to the east. Soon afterwards, in Canaan, Abram heard the Lord say, "For all the land which thou seest, to thee will I give it, and to thy seed forever" (see Gen. 13:1-15).

The Bible promises concerning land continued. Perhaps the most famous was spoken to Moses at his burning bush experience hundreds of years later: that God would deliver His people from the "hand of the Egyptians" and bring them "unto a land flowing with milk and honey" (Ex. 3:8).

That the promises at the burning bush were connected to the earlier ones was revealed to Moses. "I will bring you in unto the land, concerning the which I did swear to give it to Abraham, to Isaac, and to Jacob; and I will give it to you for an heritage: I am the Lord" (see Ex. 6:4, 8).

After the Hebrews escaped from Pharaoh, the promises were continued. "The Lord spake unto Moses, saying, Send thou men, that they may search the land of Canaan, which I give unto the children of Israel" (Num. 13:2).

Physical Or Spiritual Land?

The promises concerned both a physical and a spiritual land. The term, "promised land" has both a physical and a spiritual meaning.

"Jerusalem" is widely acknowledged as also having both a physical and a spiritual meaning in Scripture. A recent TV documentary about the Passover spoke of the physical and spiritual Jerusalem. The Bible speaks of "New Jerusalem," the holy city descending.

There's often so much overlap between the physical and spiritual in key Scriptural things and concepts that they seem to be the same.

At other times, they are clearly very different.

Those embracing only a literal Scripture may choose to stick with the physical only.

In the New Testament, we read, "By faith Abraham, when he was called to go out into a place which he should after receive as an inheritance, obeyed.... He sojourned in the land of promise...with Isaac and Jacob, the heirs with him of the same promise: for he looked for a city which hath foundations, whose builder and maker is God" (Heb. 11:8-10).

Abraham "looked for a city which hath foundations, whose builder and maker is God." There's a very spiritual sense in that statement.

Many will agree there's a spiritual sense of America, and one that is physical—and many stages in between.

The Physical State Changes When It
Encounters The Spiritual

As we study the Scriptures, we'll find a *third element* in addition to the physical and spiritual: the changed physical condition that results from encountering the divine.

After Abram and Sarai followed God's instructions and came to Canaan, they encountered angels and were told Sarai would conceive and bear Isaac (Jacob's father). They both "laughed" because Abram was 100 and Sarai ninety (Gen. 17:17), and Sarai had been barren. Nonetheless, the prediction came true.

The physical bodies of Abram and Sarai were changed by the encounter; also they received new names (Abraham and Sarah), indicative of their great spiritual progress (a concept reiterated in the Book of Revelation (2:17).

Abraham was told he'd father many nations, and that his seed (his offspring) would become as the sands of the sea.

When the time came for Isaac to marry, Abraham acted under God's instructions and sent a servant to Nahor, near Haran, where some of his family dwelt, and found Rebekah. The God-directed arrangement (she had not even seen Isaac) met with her and her family's approval, therefore she traveled back with the servant, and married Isaac.

Barren, she was healed through prayer (Gen. 25:21), and bore the twins Esau and Jacob.

Jesus later spoke of the divine realm "at hand," indicating that the realization of it had extraordinary effects. He said, "Go, preach, saying, The kingdom of heaven is at hand. Heal the sick..." (Mat. 10:7-8).

Our encounter even in a small degree with the divine reality produces healings, protections, supplyings, productive activities, and significant changes in our human nature. These and other phenomena have been exhibited throughout the Judeo-Christian saga to the present, and are the theme of this book.

The First "Israel" Was Jacob's New Name— Resulting From His Encounter With The Divine

Before his transforming session with the angel, Jacob, although not an honest man, saw the spiritual "Jacob's ladder" when on his way to his Uncle Laban's in Haran. (He'd been sent there by Rebekah his mother to escape the wrath of his brother Esau.)

In Haran Jacob, Laban, and Laban's daughter Leah all engaged in both straight and sneaky dealings.

Years later Jacob went home, taking Leah (whom Laban had snuck, disguised behind veils, into what was supposed to have been Jacob's marriage to Rachel), also her sister Rachel (his true love, whom he married after Leah), and their children. Also traveling were "two womenservants" (Bilhah and Zilpah, the maids of Rachel and Leah), who had also borne him children (with the wives' permission).

On this trip, he encountered an angel. The result was a mighty struggle with his imperfect nature, in which he was deeply changed and given by the angel the new name of "Israel," "for as a prince hast thou power with God and with men, and hast prevailed" (Gen. 32:28).

The "Promised Land"
Is The Largely-Unseen Divine Kingdom

Didn't God create the physical? Not really. God's creation is in the image of Spirit, and our progressive realization of this enables us to work our way by stages out of the flesh.

These stages take us up the "ladder" or along the Bible's "path" or "highway"—into the Promised Land.

Abraham's Connection To The
Much Later Hebrews In Egypt

Abraham's solid connection to the great Hebrew colony that later grew at Goshen in Egypt was made clear when God told him, "Know of a surety that thy seed shall be a stranger in a land that is not theirs, and shall serve them; and they shall afflict them four hundred years" (Gen. 15:13).

We know Abram first visited Egypt soon after originally reaching Canaan, and returned.

Some sources place Jewish settlements in Egypt from about 1800 B.C. (Dates aren't precise in this period, but most scholars agree on general times, although there's a wide variety of dissenting opinion as discussed later in this book).

Joseph, a great-grandson of Abraham, became Pharaoh's second-in-command (Gen. 41). Soon thereafter, Israel (Jacob) moved to Egypt in a group of "threescore and ten" (Gen. 46:27) including himself. To please Joseph, Pharaoh permitted them to settle "in the best of the land...in the land of Goshen" (47:6). This was the beginning of the great colony. They weren't subjugated until much later (Ex. 1).

The twelve tribes later enslaved in Egypt were named after the sons of *Jacob* (who had been renamed Israel).

Sons of Leah: Reuben, Simeon, Levi, Judah, Issachar and Zebulun; sons of Rachel: Joseph and Benjamin; sons of Zilpah: Gad and Asher; sons of Bilhah: Naphtali and Dan.

All were, of course, great-grandsons of Abraham and Sarah.

The Exodus

About 1250 B.C., Moses was appointed of God to lead the Hebrews out of slavery to the land He promised them.

Exodus cites 600,000-plus early fugitives counting only "men plus children." Numbers gives the same figure for males over twenty able to go to "war." Some scholars add women and still place the number at far less, the definition of the word elip, and other things, being variously interpreted.

Quantities as well as exact times for events are hard to pin down, for reasons listed below and in the next chapter.

One assumption on dates is that Abram was in Haran around 1950 B.C., and that the Exodus took place some 700 years later, circa 1250 B.C. However, scholars differ all the way down to a much shorter period.

Little Or No Writing

Regarding the 2750 years from Adam in 4000 B.C. to the Exodus in 1250 B.C. (including the Flood perhaps 2500 B.C. and Abraham 2000 B.C.), there was *only an oral history*.

From Abraham forward the oral history was partly corroborated by surrounding nations and peoples.

Until Moses wrote—or is widely considered to have written—the first five books (the Pentateuch) of Christian and Jewish Scriptures in about 1250 B.C., no Hebraic *written* record existed.

Consider that by 1250 B.C., the oral history of 2750 years had spanned a period longer than from the present time back to the Greeks.

How could information passed down orally over such a long period of time be deemed so accurate that religions could be built on it? Because it's believed that God aided in the reliability of man's writing. (Some believe every word of the Bible was dictated by God, but this writer assumes that highly inspired people, and some not so inspired, wrote down their perceptions.)

From perhaps 1500 B.C. (which was prior to the Exodus) Egypt substantiated some Hebrew history on papyrus or on temple walls and columns. In other surrounding areas, some of the corroboration is in the form of tablets, some merely in artifacts from excavations of tombs and cities, and the balance in oral histories and legends.

Better Records Kept After The Exodus

After the Exodus, most agree on basic Hebrew history with two major exceptions: one, precisely where the Hebrews crossed the body of water which parted for them but engulfed the pursuing Egyptians; and two, exactly which mountain Moses climbed to obtain the Ten Commandments.

Scholars believe a handful of crossing sites were feasible, whereas there's much more general agreement that the popular Mount Sinai is the right mountain (although even some proponents express reservations; and dissenters rule it out entirely.)

Since I regularly read three archaeology magazines, two of which focus particularly on Bible lands and topics, I don't wildly speculate in these matters, despite what might be the appearance of my suggestions below.

I submit for consideration along with other theories the interesting book, *The Mount Sinai Myth* (see bibliography) with its epilogue *claiming satellite photos* of wide, ancient trails leading across the mouth of the Gulf of Aqaba on a shallow strip located there, and asserting that to be Moses' crossing. (How could that be the "Red Sea"? Because Edom means red, and it was the Edomite Sea—apparently called Red Sea on occasion in the Old Testament.)

Interestingly, on the east side of the Gulf of Aqaba, the Arabs have closed off the area around Jabal al Lawz with wire and guards. The local Arabs have traditionally called it the mountain of Moses.

The book's author and associates made nearly undetected trips to the area, noting the shape of the mountain mass, and the peculiar black color of its top—and that these agreed with scriptural descriptions. Throughout the book, careful attention is given to Bible descriptions.

Inside the wire, they discovered other landmarks described in Scripture, including constructions believed to be the twelve pillars which Moses installed. Today these stand about level with the ground due to drifting sand, and are said to be eighteen feet in diameter.

Be all that as it may or may not be, the Hebrews brought few material assets when leaving Egypt. The Bible tells of miraculous provision of food and water when needed.

The wandering spanned forty years, and this figure seems supportable (although some believe it merely means "a long time") because the ages of the leaders apparently advanced by forty years.

Desert peoples have traditionally been nomads, so the nomadic life was not as strange or difficult as it might seem to modern readers. Also, the "desert" wasn't always the utter "wilderness" of some locations in that part of the world. The more hospitable parts (although they seldom could be called cropland) provided pasture and water for herds and people. No doubt the Hebrews camped long periods.

The Promised Land?

After Moses brought the Hebrews the second time to the Jordan River (the first was their initial inspection, when the decision was taken that they weren't strong enough to capture the land), Moses passed away. Joshua, with the Jordan parting before him, led them into what was then Canaan and today is the land of Israel.

The *physical* land was theirs, yet this was no "land flowing with milk and honey" described to Moses (Ex. 3:8). Those terms directed thought to a spiritual, present yet unseen, divine realm of which the Bible speaks in many places.

For example, Jesus later spoke of the "kingdom...hid," saying, "The kingdom of heaven is like unto treasure hid in a field; the which when a man hath found, he...buyeth that field" (Mat. 13:44).

As I see it, Jesus was telling us to seek the divine kingdom which was present but hidden. The buyer first "selleth" all that he hath, and I believe this means letting go of the material concept of things to make room for the new.

"Canaan" is another of those dual terms for solid earth and also spiritual realities, appearing in inspired hymns and sermons to this day.

The Hebrews had been led to the Promised Land; however the physical land wasn't it—the spiritual, unseen kingdom was.

After arriving and occupying the countryside (sometimes after slaughtering every man, woman, and child in captured cities), did the Hebrews then greatly decrease their search for the spiritual Promised Land?
It would appear so.
And they encountered troubles on a major scale, extending even unto this day.

Big And Continuing Trouble

The twelve tribes occupied different areas.
Collectively they encountered extreme difficulties, although they often experienced divinely-guided victories. David's kingdom around 1,000 B.C. constituted the peak of the tribes' prosperity and power. The Hebrew domain reached from the Gulf of Aqaba north far above Damascus to the banks of the Euphrates River close to the northern borders of today's Syria, yet not as far as Haran.
God protected David, his armies, and the quality of his governing. His son Solomon was known for his divinely-inspired wisdom and the building of Solomon's Temple, as well as for his many wives and life as a sensualist.
Decline followed.

Series Of Occupations By Big Empires

The Assyrians invaded first. Their vast empire under numerous kings, lasting for centuries, shrank the kingdom of David and Solomon, beginning about 850 B.C., down to a line well below Damascus. In 722 B.C., they conquered the northern kingdom, called Israel, while leaving the southern kingdom, called Judah (which included Jerusalem) with some autonomy.

Whereas maps of different phases of the nearly 300-year Assyrian Empire show general lines of expansion, they aren't precise for many reasons. A general might sweep through an area destroying opposition, then call it conquered. The main forces—or even all the forces, such as in the deserts of Libya—might then move on. Administrators and small forces might or might not remain.

Add to this the inadequacy or even total lack of records in many instances, or inaccurate accounts exaggerating the facts in order to glorify a campaign or leader.

Some areas were under thorough administration. On the other hand, at least one area—Judah —was permitted to semi-govern itself as long as it behaved.

Whereas some Middle Eastern empires ruled by crushing, others sought cooperation by giving the locals some leeway and authority. Alexander, who came much later, intermarried his men with local ladies, hoping his regime would be accepted and thus less prone to rebellions.

The Assyrians, although showing flexibility with Judah, were the first to carry Jews into captivity.

Babylon invaded next. After rebelling and joining the Medes to the north, it overthrew the Assyrians and permanently destroyed Nineveh, their capital, up the Tigris.

Then, using the "crush everything" type of governing, Babylonians entered Judah and destroyed Solomon's Temple in 586 B.C., ending the last of Jewish independence.

Following that came at least three dispersions of Jews into Babylonian captivity.

Babylon's empire covered essentially the "Fertile Crescent" from the head of the Persian Gulf up the Tigris and Euphrates Rivers past Babylon (which is south of today's Baghdad) all the way into what's now southern Turkey, then down along the Mediterranean coast through Canaan all the way into Egypt. Its most famous Bible figure was Nebuchadnezzar. Babylon wasn't a big empire, and it lasted only seventy-odd years from 612 to 539 B.C.

The Persians were next to invade and conquer, placing Jerusalem and the old Hebrew lands under yet another conqueror. Persia was the biggest Middle Eastern empire yet, stretching north and east beyond the Caspian and Aral seas to the border of India before returning west along the Arabian Sea and Persian Gulf. It covered the Fertile Crescent including Canaan, and extended over the lower Nile. In the northwest, it blanketed present-day Turkey and occupied a chunk of Macedonia.

Under biblical figures Cyrus II (the Great), Darius I, II and III, Xerxes I and II, and Artaxerxes I, II and III—not in that order—and others, the Persian Empire lasted more than 200 years. (Alexander beat Darius III at Issus in 333 B.C.)

Persian king Cyrus allowed his victims to keep some self-government, particularly their indigenous religions.

In line with this policy, he gave permission to captive peoples from all lands to return home if they wished. Some Jews went, some didn't—one source explaining they had houses and activities and were more or less content, although those remaining were supportive of those who opted to go.

Alexander was next to occupy Canaan. Young, and expecting death, he willed his empire among his top generals.

Control of Jerusalem went first to Antigonus, who got Turkey; next (by 270 B.C.) to Ptolemy, who ruled Egypt; then to the Seleucid dynasty, which had begun under Seleucus I Nicator, a young general with Alexander, in charge of the remainder of Babylon and Persia. Events were not that simple, but that was the gist of it.

Brief Return To Self-Rule

The "Hellenizing" policy coming from the Greek generals and their splits of Alexander's empire, would have stamped out Judaism except for the rise of the Maccabees, who put up a fight for Jewish religion and political freedom.

Lo, Syria recognized Jewish independence, and in 139 B.C. the *Roman Senate* did the same. The 102 years 165-63 B.C. was known as the "Hasmonean Jewish Kingdom. "

Rome

Rome, growing stronger and more aggressive, would later become bigger than the other empires at their peaks. It eventually ruled essentially everything around the Mediterranean, plus much of budding Europe and half of the British Isles in the west, also the lands of the ancient empires as far east as the Caspian Sea and head of the Persian Gulf.

This latest of iron heels first marched into Jerusalem in 63 B.C. There were many instances of significant Jewish resistance; however, all efforts failed. The Temple was destroyed by the Romans A.D. 70 after the Zealots' revolt. Sixty-five years later, Bar Kochba (or Kokhba), who had briefly reestablished Jewish independence, was defeated by Hadrian. The Diaspora or near-depopulation followed.

Not The Land Of Milk And Honey

Obviously, the Hebrew territories weren't the land of milk and honey. Those references were to a spiritual reality Jesus said we didn't see, but hoped we would.

In Lamentations we read, "Our inheritance is turned to strangers, our houses to aliens. We are orphans and fatherless, our mothers are as widows. Our necks are under persecution, we labor, and we have no rest" (5:2-3, 5).

And there were more conquerors to come: Islam, Christian Crusaders, Turks, British.

Although the physical land was not primarily the land God was directing them to, the original ordainment regarding the physical land still stands. Thus it would seem the physical land will continue to transform under the conscious presence of the divine, in the same manner Jacob did.

History Of The Temple

The special significance of Jerusalem's historic Temple above all other Jewish places of worship originates with the Ark of the Covenant. Solomon's Temple provided a home and protection for that. Furthermore, with the Temple's outer and inner court and holy of holies, it was a highly symbolic structure representing the relationship of the religion to the people and vice versa. Beautiful and imposing, it stood for grandeur and permanency.

It's said that nothing today remains of that structure, destroyed by the Babylonians in 586 B.C. (Martin Gilbert in his videotape *Jerusalem* says some now believe they've found parts of Solomon's walls in tunnels excavated under the Temple Mount.) Be that as it may, Solomon's Temple was partly restored after Jews began to return from captivity when Persia toppled Babylon and released them. This initiated the "Second Temple Period" around 538 B.C. One source says slow progress didn't produce a real structure until 517 B.C. (As for the city walls of Jerusalem, Nehemiah didn't rebuild these until about 445 B.C.)

There was at least one more destruction of the Temple before the Roman occupation 63 B.C.

After the Roman occupation, Herod the Great (the half-Jewish Roman administrator) remodeled and expanded the Temple to splendor 20-9 B.C. This structure is called the Second Temple (although this was actually the final example in the Second Temple Period). As mentioned, it was burned by the Romans in A.D. 70. The final remnant of the rebellious Zealots was extinguished after the long siege of Masada.

Today's "Western Wall" or "Wailing Wall" is a fragment of the Herod-restoration Temple, not of Solomon's or the many earlier post-Solomon efforts.

*From Jesus Onward, Jews And The New
Christians Gradually Grew Apart,
And Christians Were Soon Persecuted,
Although Later Accepted*

The separation of the new Christianity from Judaism might be said to have occurred when Paul started preaching to the Gentiles. Regardless of the time, there have always been two arguments: That the religions are indivisible and that they are separate. Most believe in a connection, an overlap, and that matters will be resolved in time.

Of course, Jesus and the disciples were both Jews and Christians, a fact making sharp separation difficult.

Peter and Paul were martyred in Rome because of Christianity, not Judaism. That bespoke a splitting off, and recognition in the Roman mind (which ruled the world of that day) of separateness.

After Jesus, the Roman Empire was progressively in turmoil both internally and on its borders despite, for a time, the "Pax Romana."

In A.D. 312, Roman emperors (and claimants) struggled internally. This was typical, almost inevitable, because the system required pairs to rule. Emperor Constantine with an army entered Italy to fight Emperor Maxentius at Rome. Seeing a vision of the cross or having a dream, or both, and hearing a voice telling him to conquer in the name of the cross, according to legends, Constantine won.

Before his death in 311, the former emperor Galerius had granted Christianity tolerance; however the 313 Edict of Milan gave all religions freedom to worship, making Christianity not just tolerated but legal. (It wouldn't become the state religion until, sources vary, 391 or 393.)

Christianity's great growth had made it the standout single religion among many pagan religions in the territories —larger even than the central Roman pagan religion with its panoply of gods with statues, temples, rituals, and festivals.

Constantine wanted Christianity's acceptance in Rome, but doubted he could obtain it without a fight since the Roman Senate was uniformly pagan. Considering these and other factors, he looked east.

Constantine co-ruled with Licinius, but the two didn't get along. Licinius even started persecuting Christians again. Constantine defeated him in battle in 323, leading to fourteen years in which Constantine was the *sole* emperor of Rome, west and east, until his death in 337.

When earlier (326) he'd chosen Byzantium as his future capital, and laid its cornerstone, he'd modestly renamed it Constantinople.

The formal date of the New Rome and seat of empire (since he was the only emperor in this period) was A.D. 330, when the city was dedicated to the Virgin Mary in an inauguration ceremony by Christian ecclesiastics.

The East's position steadily grew stronger because the West was in deepening trouble from invaders.

Would paganism regain supremacy? Julian the Apostate thought so, but his efforts around 362 didn't succeed, leaving Theodosius I (the Great) to settle the matter in 391 or 393, making Christianity the state religion.

Islamic Control Of Palestine

Mostly after Mohammed's death in A.D. 632, his followers expanded rapidly, religious zeal and military action taking over the Near East, Africa's shore, and part of Spain.

Christians Capture Jerusalem—Briefly

Christianity, resenting Islam's control of Jerusalem, launched the Crusades, and captured the city.

For a time, there existed something called the "Crusader states" along the Mediterranean, from about 1100 until nearly 1300. Then Islam was back in total control.

The Ottoman Turks knocked over Constantinople in 1453, ending the Byzantine Empire and extending the Islamic. Some say the Roman Empire terminated at this point.

Islam continued to own Palestine.

Persecutions Of Jews
By Muslims And Christians

There were forcible conversions of Jews both by Muslims in the Middle East and Christians in Europe over many centuries, causing some to choose death rather than acceptance. Most who accepted became "secret Jews" or "marranos" leading two lives: one on the surface and the other in conscience, sometimes also in underground services.

Some believe Columbus was a marrano, and that several other secret Jews were in his crew.

Jews permitted to remain Jews in Europe were sometimes forced to wear a distinctive badge or ribbon, often yellow, or special hat, dating back hundreds of years before Hitler's infamous yellow Star of David.

Both the Spanish and Roman "Christian" Inquisitions tormented Jews; and there were other burnings and tortures.

Martin Gilbert's *Atlas of Jewish History* shows hundreds of years of persecutions of European Jews, with maps of enclaves for them dating from at least 1200. (The biggest area was the huge, Russian-Polish "Pale" from the Black Sea almost to the Baltic, where they mingled of course with the other populations, while the smallest enclaves were the concentrations in various ghettos. "Pale" essentially means boundary or staked area.)

Besides concentrations, there were expulsions.

Christians have obviously not always behaved in a Christian manner.

Christians fought Christians in World Wars I and II, and in WWII added the incomprehensible dimension of a so-called "Christian" nation imposing genocide on the Jews.

The British Empire Gets Palestine

Lawrence of Arabia drove the Turks out of Palestine and other areas as a friend of the Arabs who was also an officer in the British Army. He wanted the nomadic, tribal Arabs to have their own councils and to control the old Turkish territories; however, the Arabs weren't organized or ready to work in political concert.

In peace agreements following World War I, Jerusalem was handed to the British.

Now England held Canaan Land.

Even The US Has Not Always Treated Jews Politely

Surely the Jews who made their way to the US found an open, happy place? Not so. There was anti-semitism, although it was far from universal. A shipload of Jews trying to escape Nazi Germany was turned away from the US, and also from some other western hemisphere nations, forcing them to retreat in fear to the Fatherland. It's doubtful many survived.

The US had its so-called "gentleman's agreement" excluding Jews from clubs, resorts, subdivisions—even entire towns. It had its "quotas" at colleges and elsewhere.

Raised in part around New York, the largest US Jewish community of the time, I occasionally heard some vocal opposition and slurs, but mainly saw and heard the warm relationships and cultural excellence the Jews were famous for. The city was also a big Catholic center, and large public gatherings might have at least one rabbi and one priest on the platform. The Catholic would rise and tell a harmless joke about a priest and a rabbi, and everyone would laugh, after which the Jewish gentleman would tell one about a rabbi and a priest—which again drew good-humored response. There was accommodation that recognized differences and drew smiles which indicated the onlookers realized they were silly to hold differences, because all were people.

1948 And The New Jewish State

After WWII, the Jews reestablished their home state. Forcing Britain out of Palestine, the new nation made friends with the receding British Empire.

The new Jewish state also forced out hundreds of thousands of Arabs. Peace with the Palestinians remains elusive.

The US, of course, has sided unequivocally with the new state of Israel (while balancing its need for Arab oil, and for peace in the region).

Slow Admittance Of Holocaust Into US Thought

Strangely, Hitler's gigantic wipeout of the Jews was slow to enter the US mind despite occasional news stories that made the situation plain.

The US population just didn't want to accept or think about the exterminations.

In the late Fifties, the old *True* magazine ran a story and photos almost fifteen years after the fact. Friends of mine wouldn't look at it. The nation as a whole simply wasn't ready for it.

It was at least twenty years after Hitler before we began to talk about Auschwitz and to see that "death camps" were different from "concentration camps."

In the Seventies (thirty years after the fact) death camps began to creep into our movies.

Sophie's Choice was in the Eighties, *Schindler's List* in the Nineties—at the fifty-year mark.

Is this odd? Yes, but consider that the nation as a whole also wouldn't accept other horrifying things. For example (although not in the same league as the Holocaust) it couldn't conceive of its own part in the firebombing of Hamburg and Dresden until Kurt Vonnegut's *Slaughterhouse-Five* in the Sixties (and not even then). We've never really accepted our two A-bombs into our thought, and certainly not the year-long firebombing of Tokyo which is said to have amassed a million horrible deaths.

So, whereas we're not totally "in denial" we're not totally in acceptance either, but about halfway in between.

Have The Jews Found The Promised Land?

Not yet. The physical land continues to be troubled. Today's nation of Israel has been in wars for its very life since setting up, and could be attacked in a major way internally or externally at any time.

-

What Happened To The "Lost Tribes Of Israel"?

As the result of all the dispersals from Canaan beginning with the Assyrians and culminating in A.D. 135, it's said that ten of the twelve tribes of Israel were lost.

Where did they go? They're either out there but don't know they're Jews, or have intermarried to the point that their ethnicity is submerged in other nations, peoples, cultures, and religions.

The *Atlas of Jewish History* includes maps showing where Jews relocated in various time periods, captivities, and voluntary travels.

It's known that Jews went north into what's now Russia, then east into Europe; also north and east through Turkey and Greece; also by sea to Italy, Spain and the British Isles. The presence of Jews in those areas is proof of these migrations, but doesn't explain the "lost tribes."

Within the past 200 years, a concept has emerged to show that many Europeans seeking greater freedoms in North America have actually been Jews, although not classified either by themselves or others as such.

The best map and data I've seen on the possible distribution of the lost tribes come from "Pathfinder" (see bibliography for address).

The *Atlas of Jewish History* mentions that in 1900 there were some two million persons in Europe and the US who believed Anglo-Saxons to be of the Jewish lost tribes.

If lost tribes of Israel are, in any great quantity, part of the US population, *unknown and uncounted as Jews,* this could help explain the almost mystical relationship of the US to the nation of Israel.

Whenever this relationship is discussed, we are naturally reminded of the basic Judeo-Christian connection, and that the mainly-Christian US wants to assure the well-being of the small Jewish nation which is part of a mutual tradition.

We know there are millions of identified Jews in the US.

However, are the "lost tribes," or some of them, also here—and for a spiritual purpose?

At the very least, it's interesting to think about.

With an encyclopedia of the Apocalypse plus many other books and some films appearing, there will no doubt be extensive "end-time" discussion about the lost tribes, with additional information and voluminous speculation.

-

Searchers For The Promised Land
Have Traveled On A Trail Of Blood—
And There May Be More To Come

"The Search" began with Hebrews, but can be found anywhere and with anyone in many cultures, religions, denominations, nations, economic and social classes, and ethnic groups.

It's thriving in the US "vestibule" for spiritual progress.

< >

2
THE SEARCHERS: A SEPARATE CIVILIZATION

The Hebrews as a whole were always distinctive, but the searchers were distinct even within them.

The searchers who had been changed by encounters with the divine realm comprised a civilization separate from all cultures around them, even while they dwelt within.

This pattern of double distinction was apparent when they lived (and later were enslaved) among the Egyptians, and when Assyrians, Babylonians, Persians, Greeks, and Romans came as conquerors.

Later searchers were mainly Christians (although not all Christians searched) and their quest for divine encounters and changes remained distinct within Western Civilization.

Pre-Abrahamic Jewish History
From Which The Hebrews Emerged

Bible history traces Abraham's ancestry back to Adam (about 4,000 B.C.), passing the Flood (about 2,500 B.C.).

Scripture says the pre-Flood fathers lived for centuries, also that Enoch ascended leaving no remains, and that Noah was close enough to God to be instructed to build the ark.

If these things are true, then our civilization of the miraculous began at Adam not Abraham.

Abrahamic Hebrews

However, Abraham received new instructions, ordainments and prophecies which differentiated his period and activity from the ancestral period in three main areas.

He (and his followers) were to search for the Promised Land. Second, a vast number (like earth's dust—Gen. 13: 16; and like the stars—Gen. 15:5) would come from Abraham. Jacob was told his seed would eventually bless "all the families of the earth" (Gen. 28:14). Third, the encounters with the divine, and subsequent receipt of beneficial changes, were available to the great group envisioned.

All this new stage of development greatly broadened things.

History Gives Us Five "Broadening" Occasions

The first was the divine illumination possessed by the pre-Flood fathers, and the results therefrom.

Next was Abraham's broadening shown above.

Later, Jesus broadened things by showing divine power and instructing disciples and followers to start on the path of doing divine works. Soon thereafter, this availability was broadened to include the Gentiles.

The fifth broadening relates to the modern era, of which Bible prophecy says "It shall come to pass afterward, that I will pour my spirit upon all flesh" (Joel 2:28, see also Acts 2:16-17). The full quotations, related closely to Matthew 24, indicate encounter, beneficial change, and empowerment available and practiced by everyone—by "all flesh."

Abraham's Seed As The Dust, And As The Stars, And Blessing Every Family On Earth

Were his "seed" his physical descendants or those following the spiritual ordainments? The latter, I think.

Certainly his physical seed became vast. The Jews descended from him and Sarah. The Arabs descended from him and Hagar, with Sarah's permission.

Jesus rebuked hecklers who claimed they were Abraham's seed yet sought to kill Jesus. After they insisted "Abraham is our father," Jesus said if they were Abraham's children they would do the works of Abraham (Jn. 8:37-40). It would appear Jesus meant the man wasn't a spiritual son of Abraham even if a physical descendant.

Paul said, "[Not] because they are the seed of Abraham, are they all children: but, In Isaac shall thy seed be called." Of the "children of the flesh," he said, "the children of the promise are counted for the seed" (Rom. 9:7-8).

It would make solid biblical sense if any who were inspired, empowered, and able to overcome should cover the earth in time. This would include any people anywhere who were searching, encountering, getting changes and other benefits.

In the patriarchal society and religion of ancient times, Sarah was nearly left out, whereas she was herself changed by her encounter and thereby enabled to bear Isaac in her old age, to become fifty percent of the initial generating.

As for the physical descendants, perhaps God will remind the Jews and Arabs that his promises to Abraham involved both. When battling, if they'll lift up their eyes they'll see the divine realm where everyone has everything. In Scripture, we read of the reconciliation of "Egypt," "Assyria," and "Israel": "Whom the Lord of hosts shall bless, saying, Blessed be Egypt my people, and Assyria the work of my hands, and Israel mine inheritance" (Isa. 19:21-25). But much mayhem is biblically prophesied before that time.

The Searchers Were Different From Their Own Culture

Those who were changed were different from the rest of the twelve tribes and vast numbers who followed. They were the more spiritual ones in a general population ranging down, by Bible accounts, to some very base characters including some who even opposed the advanced status.

A Few Quick Notes About Terms:

The word "Hebrew" probably came from the area's "Habiru" population stock at the time of Abraham. Today we intend the word to mean Abrahamic Hebrews. The word "Jew" comes from "Judah," a son of Jacob, whose tribe later occupied the southern kingdom named Judah in Canaan. It generally is interchangeable for "Hebrew." The biblical pre-Flood fathers were part of Jewish history, but weren't called either Hebrews or Jews at the time.

Who were the Habiru, and did the Hebrews (and not just their name) come from them?

The Bible implies a chain of generation from Adam with spiritual overtones, yet says descendants of Noah founded Babel and also Nineveh. Thus, the post-Flood biblical fathers could have produced the early Tigris and Euphrates populations, leading to those who would be called Habiru, and next to the changed and upgraded Abrahamic Hebrews.

The Searchers At Goshen Were Separate From The Egyptian Culture

The Pharaohs feared the increasing numbers, prosperity, and diligence of the Hebrews, therefore subjugated them lest they decide to take over the Nile nation.

The Searchers Continued To Be Distinct From Even Their Own People On The Exodus

Moses was a "major league" searcher under the ordainments and prophecies over him to lead the people out of bondage to the "land of milk and honey." Though his leadership was empowered by God, many followers complained, and even made and worshiped the golden calf.

The Searchers Were Separate From The Various Conquerors Of Canaan B.C.

Assyria carried off captives. These may or may not have included some searchers. Some Jews were assimilated, while others remained distinct as Jews.

Babylon is famous for having carried Jews into captivity (and for destroying Solomon's Temple). In Babylon, some Jews undoubtedly were assimilated, while others apparently retained distinctiveness, and some moved on.

Persia permitted the Jews to return from Babylon, but some were so settled they didn't come home.

Greece and its several splinter empires coming afterwards continued the pattern of reacting sharply to the general Hebrew population. "Hellenization" programs used with success elsewhere were attempted in the Jewish homeland; however, the Jews resisted, and under the Maccabees actually established independence again for a time.

Rome Reacted Harshly To The Expanding Searchers

By including power, and teaching his Jewish followers to heal, Jesus greatly broadened the awareness of what was obtainable through encounters with the divine. After he departed, disciples renewed power on the Day of Pentecost. After that, the fellowship (almost all Jewish) which was able to express divine power, was more and more identified as Christian. Paul took the message to the Gentiles.

Rome reacted brutally to what it perceived as an ever-increasing threat.

Didn't Western Civilization And The Searchers Later Become Virtually Synonymous? No, The Searchers Mingled But Were Separate

When did Western Civilization begin? If in Pericles' Athens in the 400s B.C., Abraham was busy 1,500 years earlier.

Even if one chooses Mycenaean Greece of 1450-1150 B.C., Abraham was 500 years earlier. (The legendary Odysseus was in the 1200s, the Troy campaigns in the 1100s. Eratosthenes dates the Trojan Horse at 1194.)

Some have said Olympia's games originating about 776 B.C. were a starting point.

Certainly many pre-Athenian activities were tributaries, but it's Periclean Athens that seems to be the most suitable start for Western Civilization.

Pericles led a semi-democracy and enunciated the concept still growing in popularity, that "Power rests with the majority instead of a few." He also rebuilt the Acropolis, and built the Parthenon.

However, before Pericles, descendants of Abraham (1950 B.C.) had developed as a people, left Egypt (1250 B.C.), searched for the biblical land, built David's kingdom (1000 B.C.), been invaded by Assyrians, Babylonians, and Persians, and returned from captivity to partly rebuild their Temple.

Note also that Jewish history in contrast to Greek included searchers for the Promised Land whereas Greece had none of record.

Too, the Hebrews were at least officially monotheistic, while Greece was pagan with many gods.

Note: At this point in the chapter, we've moved out of the most ancient times into "A.D."

Below is a special section discussing indefinite and even conflicting information regarding many ancient dates, ages, and events. It will particularly trace the development of general writing and Hebrew writing for the early Bible.

-

(Special Section)
WHY WAS THERE SO MUCH IMPRECISION
IN EARLY HISTORY? THE BASIC REASON
WAS LACK OF WRITING

One Scholar Calls Differences In Dates And Ages,
Vagueness And Scantiness Of All Records, Lack Of
Preservation, And Other Problems Of
Historical Accuracy, Plain "Frustrating"

History books covering happenings before 1000 B.C. frequently give conflicting opinions regarding dates, ages, events, locations, and periods of time spent here and there.

We have super-sincere experts, but they often have to choose between two or even more well-supported viewpoints, and other distractions. Therefore, one often sees "circa" and sometimes much broader qualifiers such as, for instance, "some say as much as two hundred years earlier."

David Daiches, in his *Moses,* mentions biblical references to "400 years," "four generations," and "three generations," as talking about the exact same span.

The biblically-indicated long time from Abraham to Moses (accepted by many to be about 700 years from 1950 B.C. to 1250 B.C., much of which period the Israelites spent in Egypt), is contrasted to other Bible texts telling of Moses' descent from Levi (a son of Jacob) as Levi's great-grandson, which would indicate a much shorter time in Goshen for the early prosperity and the later captivity.

Egypt's history, while confirming the Hebrew presence and a few important approximate dates, doesn't deal with the matter of arrival.

Regarding ages, disturbing to me from my own re-
search is the text that Abram was seventy-five years old
before leaving Haran (Gen. 12:4), and Sarai ten years
younger (Gen. 17:17). That would have made Sarai at least
sixty-five when Pharaoh thought she was "very fair," and
"entreated Abram well for her"—offered livestock and
servants for his "sister," which is what Abram had called
her. (In fact, she was his half-sister.) So I suspect a little
flattery may have been added later for the record? If not,
then the entire system of ages of the individuals might have
to be restudied yet another time, and even revised.

Everyday Life depicts Sarah as a young, good-looking
gal in two paintings of leaving Ur on the way to Haran.

Britannica (1962) also questions dates regarding the
patriarch. It says the current biblical text is a compilation
from four books condensed into one; also that "a generation" was 100 years in one concept, forty in another; and
furthermore that a governing rule in the compilations was to
determine 1200 years from Abraham to Solomon's Temple,
whereas 600 would be more like it. The particular *Britannica* article likes 1550 to 1450 B.C. for Abraham.

Abraham's apparent reproductive powers were astonishing. Sarah died at 127 (Gen. 23:1-2), which would have
made Abraham 137. After that, he married Keturah, who
bore him six children (Gen. 25:1-2). He died at 175 (Gen.
25:7-8). Mebbe so.

Three Types Of Records

Scholars address disparities usually by making their
careful choices, and preparing to defend them.

At the same time, some scholars point out that there appear to be three types of oral accounts recorded: sacred or ritual history (which might be "shined up" a bit); tribal "saga" (prone to exaggeration); and finally precise records.

Do such different types of records impugn the Bible? No, because the Spirit of God comes through and gives us an inspired sense. In that context, whether Abraham was in 1950 B.C. or 1650 B.C. is important but not critical, and certainly we all hope to eventually have perfect information.

Some Major Answers Still Sought

Some day, the exact crossing of Moses will be found when Egyptian chariots are discovered on the bottom.

As for Noah, who long preceded Abraham, there are several credible reports of a large ship broken up in Ararat ice shifts. Not convinced, some (even while believing in the ark) point out that the bird returned with an olive branch that had been above water, and which cannot found high on a mountain.

The Macro Outline Of Hebrew History Is Not Challenged

All agree that the basic Hebrew *story* from Abraham to Jesus indisputably took place, despite areas of disagreement on dates, ages, places, and some events.

The macro Hebrew outline is confirmed by archaeological evidence and writings both where the Hebrew tribes lived and in similar records (such as they were) uncovered in neighboring lands.

To Get An Idea Of The Difficulties Historians
Face, Let's Trace The Development Of Writing

The invention of writing, all sources agree, occurred in Sumer, and consisted at first of indentations from wedge-tipped styli in mud tablets to create marks for counting and pictographs for language. In *Everyday Life In Bible Times*, the National Geographic Society puts the date at 5,000 years ago (3000 B.C.), while TIME-LIFE says a bit earlier.

Where is Sumer? Around Ur, in the southern part of Mesopotamia. It's famed also for Gilgamesh (about 2,700 B.C.), also the ziggurat built later by King Ur-Nammu, and as the place from which Abram departed around 2000 B.C.

Everyday Life says Ur-Nammu, about 2000 B.C., produced the first law code, written on tablets in cuneiform pictographs. (Schools in my youth taught that the first law code was by Hammurabi of Babylon about 1750 B.C.)

For a quick overview of Mesopotamian writing, I recommend the chapter in TIME-LIFE's *Great Ages Of Man —Cradle of Civilization* entitled "The Literate Man." Three types of cuneiform writing are explained in laymen's terms. These represent three languages: Old Persian, Elamite, and Akkadian—the last also called Assyrian or Babylonian, and considered *Semitic*.

In Search Of Hebrew Writing
Used In Scripture

The Semitic language was regional, with different dialects. Mesopotamian impressions in mud tablets developed into an early system for setting down parts of the language.

So how did humans get from the primitive stage to the comprehensive Hebrew writing? Hang on.

There were three major developments of cuneiform (matching the above three spoken languages): Old Persian with only some forty symbols (in a kind of early phonetic alphabet), the Elamite with more than 100 symbols, and the Akkadian with hundreds. (This last led through much time and many improvements from the crude clay marks to Hebrew writing.)

Pictographic symbols (comprised of marks) might be the actual thing depicted (for example, a cow), or could stand for an emotion (such as a weeping eye), or an idea, where the symbols were called ideographs, or a sound.

The complex symbols were difficult both to produce and read, being pushed into clay, or chiseled into stone tablets, or onto the bases of statues and faces of walls. Largely immobile, these were hard to drag to classrooms for teaching purposes.

Practicality increased somewhat when the basic teachings such as law, mathematics, science, and medicine were copied onto clay tablets for distribution to schools. Even with this progressive step, very few people became "literate," and those who did naturally constituted the elite. The mass was totally left out.

The symbols became more and more numerous and complicated—a pictographic system. Meanwhile, no one had yet conceived of a phonetic alphabet out of which one could make *words* representative of *anything*.

(Note: Cuneiform writing remained an impenetrable code until Carsten Niebuhr and Henry Rawlinson in the 1800s finally cracked it. Many others, working amidst mountains of old tablets and fragments, contributed vitally.)

"Meanwhile Over In Egypt...."

TIME-LIFE's scholars put the Nile's earliest picto-graphs at about 3100 B.C., saying that was *after* Mesopotamia. If so, is Sumer's first date 3200 B.C. not 3000?

Egyptian hieroglyphics, which originally represented only things, ideas, and some words, soon included *a few phonetic sounds,* helping to string together symbols to express thoughts. Lacking vowels, though, these only approached being an alphabet.

A Speedier Writing Form
Was Needed

Very early, the Egyptians became the first to develop a "speed style" suitable for general communications: the hieratic or priestly system.

On papyrus sheets with a reed pen, or on wood with a brush, both in lampblack, this faster method (which was used secularly as well) traces its appearance back almost as far as hieroglyphics.

Helping this was the early existence of the famous Egyptian papyrus "paper." While Mesopotamia was basically stuck in its mud tablets, Egypt had writing paper. Since the climate was dry, many sheets have survived to this day.

(Much later, around 700 B.C., the even faster demotic form of writing was developed and used in Egypt, but by then, Hebrew writing had long been in existence.)

Egypt, as Mesopotamia, used everything from mere marks for recording amounts of grain traded or stored, or the sizes of fields, all the way up to elaborately-decorated walls, monuments, and documents with hieroglyphics and art often exaggerating the victories of rulers who paid for them.

Between the simple marks and mighty monuments came the "written" correspondence and school texts.

Mobility Of Papyrus Sheets
Increased By Copying

Monuments aren't mobile, and tablets are clumsy. Papyrus was mobile and furthermore could get in circulation when reproduced by copyists.

As for duplicating dried mud tablets over in Sumer, the original might have been filed under 10,000 others. Oh, well, what were slaves for, anyway? "Hey you! Get that— uh...let's see...was that thirteen years ago? Or eight? You remember, don't you?—it was brown—that tablet on...."

For most centuries, and in most cases, only the original record of any data or example of writing was available.

Different languages between what were relatively small nations in the Middle East posed an additional barrier to communications. Even where "Semitic" was one basic language, the dialects were different and literacy low.

Compare those times to today when documents flash around the world in seconds, with simultaneous translation.

Getting A Grasp On Hebrew
Bible Writing

The Hebrew written records began, most say, about 1250 B.C. (although some say later, around David's kingdom 1,000 B.C., and even after that).

There were several Semitic languages, no doubt with plenty of overlap.

For our purposes in this chapter, Semites were eastern or western. Aramea (just north of Canaan) was western. Although Abram had started from the eastern area where several languages were spoken, he apparently easily shifted into the western Semitic.

Egyptian documents as early as the 1500s B.C. reveal more than 1,200 Semitic words, according to the *Encyclopedia Britannica*. These showed that a speedier writing was constantly advancing.

Cuneiform Couldn't Handle
The Languages And Vocabularies
That Were Rapidly Developing

Cuneiform was too awkward to handle the rapid expansion of languages and the progress of communications, science, construction, math, transportation, trade, and so on.

The situation was ripe for the appearance of an alphabet from which to create, using only a handful of characters instead of hundreds of complex symbols, unlimited numbers of words expressing anything, and offering the potential of stringing words together to express and explain.

The All-important Alphabet Was Coming,
And Here Were The Steps

Amongst even the earliest pictogram groupings were a few symbols representing *sounds*. "Ca" might have been a sound with its own pictogram, but the concept of combining this with other sounds to make a *word* hadn't arrived yet.

The "need for speed" led to "shorthand"—the stream-lining or metamorphosing of pictograms to make them easier to write. New materials (for example, Mesopotamia got some papyrus) popularized writing, creating more demand for easier systems.

Meanwhile, the centuries-long revolution advanced the concept of language as *sounds* from which written words could be constructed to describe *any* object, emotion, or thought.

Wilfred Funk's *Word Origins* says all alphabetic symbols originated in pictograms streamlined for quick use.

Very gradually, the development of words forced thousands of clumsy pictograms first to the sidelines and then into retirement.

The revolution was among scribes and scholars who gradually realized the emerging alphabet would open new worlds, not just process the past more efficiently. A future bulging with complexities as well as the need for subtle nuances could be accommodated with the new system.

In all this, *hundreds of years passed.*

The ancient governmental powers faded or fell, but the developing languages and systems of writing continued to emerge and upgrade with time.

Phoenician Script Or Alphabet

While cuneiform was going out of business by degrees, the *"Phoenician script"* or alphabet progressively appeared, *Britannica* tells us. It was called the "common alphabet of the western Semites," including Hebrews, Phoenicians, and Arameans. This is doubly interesting to us today because improved forms eventually became our alphabet.

The Phoenician alphabet made its way through Anatolia (Turkey) to Greece, where more vowels were added and other changes made. "West Greek" continued westward to stimulate Latin, from which came Modern European, or the final form of our "A-B-Cs." The entire subject of alphabets was more complex, but the above is a "quick handle."

Is there a connection between "Phoenicia" and "phonetics"? Not according to Funk, who says "phone" is a Greek word meaning "sound," and that the sound-system probably received its name there, although it is identified first with Phoenicia.

The Hebrew Language And Writing—
Which Writing Gave Us The Old Testament

We've seen that the Hebrew *language* developed as one of the many Semite languages popular in the Near East and changing constantly over the centuries.

Western Semitic, Canaanite Semitic, Aramaic, and Hebrew, spoken and written, were apparently all so close that scholars have problems separating them.

"Biblical Hebrew" Writing

Because the early Old Testament scrolls constitute the main Hebrew documents, the writing found there is our record of Hebrew writing.

From this has come the term, "Biblical Hebrew."

Later, some of the Bible was written in Aramaic. Still later, much was translated into Aramaic.

Along the way, Aramaic became a sort of "universal language" of the Mideast, although there were dialects of it. The general Aramaic language and writing held up until replaced much later by the Arabic.

The Hebrew of the early Bible was written on sheepskin or goatskin parchment with brushes and lampblack. The writings in many of these scrolls became part of our Jewish, Catholic and Protestant Bibles.

Moses was reputed to have written—or dictated—the first five books of the Bible, known as the Pentateuch, around 1250 B.C.   These are essentially the Jewish Torah. There are different opinions as to the date, and whether the words were perhaps written down well after Moses' passing.

Proof Today Regardless Of Historical Differences

I believe the substance of the Bible will have to be *proven* today. Jesus said we would do his works.

A single divine healing is a small flash of light from an infinite, higher realm, proving the essence of the Scriptures and bespeaking more to come, whether the precise date of an ancient event is settled or not.

The simple fact that we possess the Scriptures today— Jewish, Catholic and Protestant Bibles—is proof of divine power. When one considers how texts had to be preserved through the centuries against worms, water, mold, fire, wars, drastic political changes, and hand-copyings—and that editions were produced, selections and rejections made—the perpetuation is nothing short of miraculous.

Retained texts met further editings through the years, also small additions, deletions, or adjustments tending to reinforce the positions of the particular theologians supervising the copying and preservation. Like "point shaving," just a little here and there can affect the game.

From the beginning, plain guesswork filled in missing places in scrolls, usually shown in italics.

Since the advent of movable type, there have been translations and more editions. In the Twentieth Century alone, editions, revisions, translations, and interpretations have proliferated.

We probably all agree that the whole procedure from original writing through long preserving, and all the people who contributed, are owed a debt of gratitude.

"What can we prove today?" is going to become more and more important.

We're now in a scientific age—an age of proof. Is there a higher realm and identity? Can we encounter it? And when we do, does our human nature and condition beneficially change as the Bible shows? If so, then a few gaps or conflicting statements in historicity—while lamentable— won't matter.

TO REFOCUS, THEN, ON THE SEARCHERS' TREK:

They Went West

While mixing with Western Culture, our searchers trended westward like a plant turning towards the light.

Islam Barred The Near East To The West

After the death of Mohammed (A.D. 632), at the beginning of Islam's major expansion, the Islamic world gradually shut out the West, even while expanding into Spain. Parts of the Mideast still resist Western influence.

Ever Westward

Christianity and Judaism both trended westward. In Christian Europe, Jews had their usual struggle for place.

In time, the searchers crossed the Atlantic, moving west with an inspiration not seen since Moses left Egypt.

The expectation of additional revelation was added.

When the Pilgrims set forth in the *Mayflower,* John Robinson, their clergyman, said to them, "If God reveals anything to you by another instrument, be as ready to receive it as ever you were to receive any truth by my ministry; *for I am persuaded that the Lord has more truth yet to break out of His Holy Word.* " (Italics added).

The *Mayflower* Puritans in 1620 carried the torch for the searchers.

Of course, they weren't the first searchers to reach North America. Surely some were in all the earlier groups. Columbus came in the late 1400s. The Spanish were in the Caribbean and Florida in the first half of the 1500s. Cortés took Mexico, DeSoto explored what would later become the southern US, Coronado roamed the southwest, and Cabrillo visited parts of California. St. Augustine was founded fifty-five years before the Pilgrims landed.

Nevertheless, the *Mayflower* voyagers were the most conscious of their spiritual orientation. They (as others) believed they'd occupy a new physical land and also look— in one degree or another—for the Higher Land. They wanted to carry forward the hopes of Christianity and find religious freedom (or at least, freedom for their religion). And they were charged to look for additional revelation.

Many Puritans

When researching for this book, I was surprised to find that 67,000 Puritans emigrated from England (where they weren't popular with the powers). *Atlas Of American History* shows that before 1650, 17,800 went to New England, 9,500 to Maryland and Virginia, and about 40,000 to Bermuda and the West Indies.

Certainly not all were possessed of the Vision, and probably some (as some of other groups) had lesser expectations ranging from escape from oppression (even from jails), to material gains, to religious freedoms (although that term sometimes included oppression of other religions).

The Spanish to the south were more materialistic— incursions into what is present-day Mexico being militaristic and oriented on gold. They also credited God.

Their courage in exploring parts of what later became both the US Southeast and Southwest was a remarkable plus.

The original settlement of California seemed to be a mixture of the undeniable spirituality expressed in the missions and the material drive for gold and gain.

Three centuries afterwards, "gold fever," not spiritual vision, would pull many eastern Americans westward.

"American Dream" Or American Vision?

We hear of the "American Dream," and equate it to material wealth, houses, cars. But if all can't share in this, and we have to build walls around "exclusive communities," then we haven't got the spiritual thing, only another material phase with which history is littered.

If, as Jesus told us, a man's life doesn't consist of "the things that he possesseth," then of what doth it consist?
"Eye hath not seen, nor ear heard, neither have entered into the heart of man, the things which God hath prepared for them that love him" (Paul, in I Cor. 2:9). These things are spiritual.

The "American Vision" is the real American goal—the fulfillment of the "Search for the Promised Land."

The "Vision" Drew Many Across The Plains

There was "something" about the massive move across the Great American West.

When the US grew mightily by the 1840s, there began a decades-long surge westward which overran the Indians (a great American tragedy) but was so powerful and so certain that John Louis O'Sullivan wrote his famous "manifest destiny" comment in 1845.
In the West, countless people experienced, and experience today, a closeness to God.
The Indians' strong sense of the Great Spirit was often evident.

A Strange Thing Happened In California—
That Land Of Wonder

When the Search could no longer move west without leaving the ordained US, there was nowhere to go but up.

As if to so indicate, the trees reached to the sky. Were they pointing thought to the divine realm, higher than the material, but present?

In the 1960s, down in the desert, I stood looking at the great mountain sentinels, San Gorgonio and San Jacinto, standing guard over the pass leading into the City of Angels. A few miles behind me were camels and date palms.

I had an inspired vision of being in Bible lands, but in modern times.

Here was Israel—and what was it doing here?

Later I read a book by one of the great Pentecostal revivalists of the turn of the century, and was astounded at the writer's similar experience in the area.

As of this writing, much of that US desert is shopping centers, housing, golf courses. And the City of Angels is certainly not presently fit for the kingdom of God!

So we're talking about a spiritual sense—present although little seen.

In the US, the searchers found a land with spiritual overtones confirming it was the vestibule for finally gaining the higher revelation sought by millions for millennia.

< >

3
DIVINE HEALING: EARLY, "NIGHT," AND THE PRESENT

Jesus instructed his disciples and other followers to heal, saying, "He that believeth on me, the works that I do shall he do also" (Jn. 14:12).

However, he warned of an upcoming interruption, saying, "I must work the works of him that sent me, while it is day: the night cometh, when no man can work" (Jn. 9:4-5).

Today, divine healing is once more among us.

Early Christian Healing: Pentecost Forward

After Jesus ascended, the disciples received the power to heal and the power to convert, when they were filled with the Holy Spirit on the first Christian Day of Pentecost.

The early Christians didn't have a church in the structural or organizational sense. Their basic concept was the meeting, or "assembly." I call these, who were involved with healing and the gifts of the Spirit, the "Early Christian Fellowship."

Jesus had said, "Lo, I am with you alway" (Mat. 28: 20). That implies a closeness.

The closeness, even the fellowship, between divinity and worshipers, was essential to healing, just as the encountering of higher reality was the key to Jacob's transformation.

The New Testament mentions "the fellowship of his Son Jesus Christ our Lord" (I Cor. 1:9). And "the fellowship of the mystery, which from the beginning of the world hath been hid in God" (Eph. 3:9). Also, the "fellowship of his sufferings" (Phil. 3:10—of which we're reminded in Rev. 19:11-13 near the "end"). Too, "the fellowship with us: and truly our fellowship is with the Father, and with his Son Jesus Christ" (I Jn. 1:3).

In The Atmosphere Of Spiritual Closeness With Christ, Healings Occurred

God's direct presence without intermedial people or rituals brought healings, protections, deliverances from jails and attackers, deep psyche-changeovers, and so on.

The Slow Change To Stand-ins For An Absent *Christ*

An intermedial level began to appear almost from the start, when worshipers viewed the disciples as closer to Jesus because they had been with him. They didn't understand his promised presence, or feel adequate to relate directly.

The first intermedial level slowly placed the disciples between the average person and Deity, even in the position of *standing in for Jesus*.

Soon it was easy to believe any pastor stood closest to God, and in an intermedial position.

The growth of this concept through the centuries became the "vicar" or vicarious priest standing in for Deity.

The Rise In Intermedial Elements Over The Early Centuries Resulted In The Decline Of Divine Healing

Divine healing had occurred in the direct relationship to Deity—just as Jacob was changed in his direct encounter.

However, healing began a slow decline in proportion to the perception that the Word was coming down through priest, church, doctrine, ritual, symbol and so on, and that prayers were channeled up through the same.

The more the intermediate structure increased, the more divine healing decreased.

Pyramidal Church

At a time when there was only one minister per congregation (and some of those were pastors in the sense of not being intermedial figures), direct worship was plentiful.

(Note: Regarding the term, "bishop," apparently two concepts were involved. Where each church had its own bishop, this was not in the sense of hierarchical officials over groups of churches. However, that soon began changing.)

Congregations were scattered, and communications between churches were difficult, requiring donkey rides of several days. Rapid growth in the early centuries resulted in diversity when uniformity seemed more desirable.

The word "universal" or "catholic" appeared long before Nicaea (A.D. 325); however, it's not likely that anything as large as the later Catholic Church was envisioned at first.

As the concept of an organized church grew through the centuries, more and more pyramidal layers were added.

Night

As direct worship disappeared, divine healing disappeared, and "night" fell for "works" after A.D. 300, around Constantine.

Throughout the ages after Emperor Constantine, divine healing was hidden and sporadic. There are credible reports of results by gifted and prayerful people, but my point is that the activity was localized, small, and not continuous; and Jesus himself had predicted the break.

Awesome Persecutions By Rome In The Early Times—But Why?

The rapidly-expanding and different new Christian sect was persecuted because it represented the potential to "overcome the world" (Jesus, Jn. 16:33).

Just as Herod had killed the babes lest one grow up to topple him, authorities uneasily eyed the new movement and often attacked it.

Paul in his travels had to assure nervous government administrators that he represented no overthrow. In fact, he told his followers to pray for those in power.

Although Paul was undoubtedly a revolutionary, he knew that God's changes come in ways that bless—that beneficially replace, not destroy in the typical sense.

In this line, when he and Silas were put in prison for "teaching customs not lawful," and they prayed and sang to God at midnight, an earthquake shook the doors open and loosed the prisoners' bands. The jail keeper, fearing that his superiors would kill him if the prisoners escaped, started to commit suicide. Seeing this, Paul said, "Do thyself no harm: for we are all here" (Acts 16).

Rome was master of the western world and yet was afraid of the Christians. It could sense their access to unseen, divine power that produced changes. In addition, Rome feared any preaching which flatly predicted a new kingdom coming to earth.

Such things were seditious, encouraging rebellion.

Rome's reaction was cruel. In the first century A.D. alone, it martyred Peter (crucified upside down) and Paul in the city. (Some say Paul didn't die in Rome, others say he was beheaded there.) Christians were thrown to the lions for sport before huge crowds, and generally forced underground into the catacombs. Nero blamed the great fire on Christians. And so on.

But these and other attempts to stamp out Christianity only produced greater numbers of followers.

Was Constantine A Christian?

Roman Emperor Constantine won his big battle in 312 after seeing his vision, dream, or both, of the cross. Following that, he embraced Christianity, helped give it legal status, and put an end to most of its persecution by the state. However, he wasn't baptized (one source says "converted") until his deathbed in 337. Thus he may not have been a Christian by standard measures.

Since he won battles in the name of the Cross, many assume he was a Christian in his heart. Of course, Jesus wasn't a battle leader.

I believe Constantine's heart was political—not in a bad sense, and probably in a good way in this case.

He saw a vigorous, growing Christianity in Jerusalem, Anatolia (Turkey), Greece, the Balkans, Alexandria, Rome and elsewhere, whereas the other religions were fragmented, different from each other, local, pagan.

He realized Christianity could be a "natural fit" for him —a large and popular religion to go with his expanding view of empire.

Nicaea Looming

However, Christianity wasn't without differences, divisions, and local influences.

The emperor needed a standardized church so that when he said "Christians" all would know what he meant. Therefore he convened the famed council at Nicaea in 325.

Several hundred bishops attended. (Perhaps by this time, each spoke for multiple congregations.)

At the conference, the Arians' position was tossed out while the Caesarean position of Eusebius was accepted but with Alexandrian modifications. The result was a bit of a camel—a horse designed by a committee—and no one went away entirely satisfied, reports say.

Nonetheless, the decision stood, and Christianity followed the Nicene decisions and the developing Creed.

Divine healing, once at the very center, wasn't to be found in the new picture—in the trends, structure, Creed, or budding Church.

With Divine Healing Left Behind,
Christianity Was Now Acceptable To Rome

Christianity became tolerable because it was no longer a threat to "overcome the world."

The Early Christian Fellowship Demised

The Christianity of Peter and John on the Day of Pentecost, and for the immediate decades and centuries following, finally demised after a long decline when Christianity became a State-sponsored Church during Constantine's reign.

It's plain that the Early Christian Fellowship wasn't the same as the Church which had gradually grown in its midst, steadily supplanting it.

There's no continuum from, "Heal the sick, cleanse the lepers, raise the dead, cast out devils" (Mat. 10:7-8), to the new non-healing church.

Catholics Now And Then

God bless the Catholics—they have much to recommend them. For one thing, we'd have no Bible today were it not for consecrated preservation and copying by monks.

I have great admiration for the dedicated nursing nuns and small-parish priests.

I had a friend who wouldn't affiliate with any religion, yet said, "If I were to do so, it would be with the Catholics. I was raised in Miami, where in the worst parts of town, the church was open twenty-four hours a day." (That may not be the case today, with such disrespect in inner cities.)

Pope John Paul II is an outstanding humanitarian.

The institution deserves praise for its courageous 1960s Vatican II dropping all persecution of other religions.

However on the debit side in the old days, the Church so deeply entwined itself with states that, over the centuries, it was often difficult to tell which really ruled.

Also, ancient grossness culminated in the Spanish and Roman inquisitions in the 1400s and 1500s—and no one defends either the concept or practices.

Healing And Change Restored Today

Today, divine healing and other changes resulting from encountering the higher realm in varying degrees are back in the world to stay (Jn. 14:25-26), more widespread than ever.

Protestants led the return, but Catholic Pentecostals and Charismatics operate freely today with the blessing of the Vatican.

With divine healing and related progress comes the power to eventually change the entire world—as prophesied by Jesus and set forth in Revelation.

This power is benevolent and—this time—irresistible.

The period of "night" is over.

So do we "walk on the water" tomorrow?

No—kindergarten first, grad school later; but the higher realm, and the realization that the age of the broadest biblical possibilities has arrived, is present.

< >

4
CLIMBING THE "ISRAEL" LADDER—"JACOB'S LADDER"

Jacob's Ladder

Fleeing to Haran after cheating his brother Esau, but long before his transformative experience and new name of "Israel," Jacob dreamed of a ladder reaching to heaven with the angels of God ascending and descending on it (Gen. 28:12).

This ladder of God is available for any of us all the time.

No matter what trouble we're in, mental or physical, the "ladder" (symbolizing a way or a path out) is there if we look for it.

David wrote, "If I ascend up into heaven, thou art there: if I make my bed in hell, behold, thou art there. If I take the wings of the morning, and dwell in the uttermost parts of the sea; Even there shall thy hand lead me, and thy right hand shall hold me" (Ps. 139:8-10).

The ladder reaches us even if we don't deserve it. That's a miracle from which other miracles follow.

Jesus said, "He maketh his sun to rise on the evil and on the good, and sendeth rain on the just and on the unjust" (Mat. 5:45).

The ladder stands for what's there all the time for everyone.

Jesus told Nathanael, "Ye shall see heaven open, and the angels of God ascending and descending upon the Son of man" (Jn. 1:51). That's reminiscent of Jacob's ladder, which also had angels going up and down.

Therefore, Jesus' remarks take us farther into what this "ladder" is all about—spiritual climbing, by degrees, by stages, in the Lord.

Jesus—"the way"—shows us the progressive steps to a higher consciousness, higher power, higher form.

Climbing produces revelation after revelation, change after change. As Paul said, "We all...beholding...the glory of the Lord, are changed into the same image from glory to glory, even as by the Spirit of the Lord" (II Cor. 3:18).

Our progress is by degrees, not all at once.

In Isaiah, we read, "For precept must be upon precept...line upon line...here a little...there a little" (28:10).

Why Not Just Run To The Top?

We improve by steps as we go up, and progressively higher encounters require changes in us.

We resist change. We don't emerge from the flesh without a struggle.

Spiritual inspirations can challenge our plans and ambitions, making them seem limited and even obsolete in light of the revelation of what God has already done.

Too, inspirations can expose such things as selfishness, impurity, and greed, causing us to react, dig in our heels, and pridefully hang onto the old.

We may discover we have deep-rooted sensualism that yields only a little at a time.

The past clings to us, and we to the past.

And we may say, "heal me, but don't change me."

The circumscribed, separated nature of our mortal "I" changes as we climb. Sometimes kicking and screaming, it yields to the presence of God as the divine I AM, and to what He is showing us of our identity in His image.

In what might be likened to the angels "descending," the word keeps coming irregardless of our positive or negative reactions.

Jesus spoke of it falling like seed—some to start growing, some to have weak roots, or be eaten by birds (Mat.13: 18-23). We get new opportunities because it's always there.

Can't Skip A Rung

If we skip a rung in our climb, or any requirements of each step or group of steps, our advance will be slowed or even stopped at some point until we take care of business.

I've often had to go back and fill in spots, and no doubt still have others yet to do.

Proof Required Of Us

Testing times in our mortal life are both opportunities and requirements for us to prove divine life.

After we've proven a stage of progress for ourselves, at some point we have to use what we've learned to help others.

If we get healings and protections far ahead of where we are on the ladder, someday we have to learn the "how" of such things, and how to help others with that information.

Divine Power

With the Holy Ghost comes divine *power* (Acts 1:8). Peter and John went forth from the first Christian Day of Pentecost to exercise both dramatic healing power and the power to convert.

In our experience, power may only be the ability to control our temper in traffic; or it may be a great healing ministry, or anything in between.

In any event, the pattern of receiving power and helping others was shown in Jesus' relationship with his disciples, and we find this pattern repeated in varying degrees in the lives of millions since.

Healing Capability Appears
As We Climb The Ladder

Climbing brings us naturally into the realm of God's healing power. As climbers, we see healing, or degrees of it, as we are changed. The more we realize the great potential of God's healing and changing power, the more we use it for ourselves and others.

For many of the ladder's initial rungs, spiritual inspiration may be mixed with material healing methods, achieving excellent results, as many will attest.

Today there are more medical professionals than ever praying for healing, and amenable to working with praying people on cases.

As we climb higher and progressively recognize the spiritual as the divine reality capable all by itself of changing lives and bodies, the more the material drops away.

Still higher, if one is adequately conscious of the divine power, material therapies are left off in order for "ladder progress" to continue.

If one isn't ready for a step—and this goes for activity in any field—one shouldn't take that step. And it's very individual. No one can tell another what to do.

Mistakes are made when human willpower instead of divine guidance directs.

Two Healing Bases

Jesus' overcoming of death logically exhibits the power we seek for our own overcoming of evil, and the path in which to walk as we follow him out.

Many healings today are based on Jesus' death rather than his overcoming of death—on his "stripes" in the sense of his taking a beating instead of overcoming a beating.

Working with a God whose only will could be good gives us a sure power beyond pleas and hopes, no matter how righteous and sincere (and often rewarded) those are.

Two Major Levels

A lot of Christian healing addresses the patient as if mortality was his or her fundamental condition, asking for divinity to be bestowed upon it—often with good results on parts of the ladder.

Another level brings divine identity and reality into our experience as our fundamental condition, and applies these to mortality—with sure results.

Christian Healing, Having Returned To The Scene, Will Again Become Central To Christianity

Once central to earliest Christianity, later opposed by general Christianity, divine healing today has at least been partly accepted again. In time, it will be found in its original position.

In the end-time, wonders *not* divine are also biblically predicted. As real divine power gains, counterfeit presentations will surely increase, fooling even "the elect," if that "were possible" (Mat. 24:24).

Climbers Get Hit By Backlash To Their Ladder Progress

When we exercise divine power (or, sometimes, just stand up and be counted with it), we often get "knocked on our ass." At the very least, we get challenged.

We must handle any such backlash and, if hurt, heal ourselves—and thus solidly claim our rung and be ready for more progress.

Spiritual climbers have always met opposition.

Ancient kings didn't want to hear of power or even

knowledge greater than theirs, often killing those who represented such things. (Although they kept advisors who were supposed to have greater specialized knowledge, if the advice turned out to be bad—*zap!)*

Daniel was sent to the lions' den merely for praying to a God higher than the king, and the Children of Israel were sent to the fiery furnace for refusing to bow to a false deity.

The limits for both mind and matter were "chiseled in stone"—that is, on gravestones and dungeon walls—by kings and priests.

One of the utter boundaries was clearly the claim by the old absolute-authority kings (not like today's tame parliamentary monarchs) to be the only *ruler.* Jesus told of a higher kingdom, and his acts displayed higher *powers*—things which aroused opposition of the most violent sort.

Jesus' mere birth became such a threat to Herod the Great (when he heard the prophecy that somewhere in his kingdom was born a male child who would be king of the Jews) that he slew all male children two years and under. An angel warned Joseph and Mary, who took Jesus to Egypt.

In psychology, the father's fear—sometimes murderous—of the young son who will someday "replace" him or maybe just exceed him, is today called "Herodism."

The Past As Backlasher

Control from the past may seem odd in an age where we eagerly expect the next revolution in electronics and more changes in our lives. Once deeply entrenched and possessed of terrible power, such things as ancestral control, tradition, the authority of parents or mere age, "establishment" knowledge, and so on—have waned.

When did the reorientation from past to future occur? It's been increasing since the rebellious Sixties.

When kids instinctively understood computers, "age," which didn't comprehend, was on its way to taking a back seat.

When spiritual thought glimpsed light ahead (whereas it had formerly believed divine heights and wisdom were in the past), orientation changed.

The unsettled conditions in concepts of family, sex, entertainment, and so on, which resulted from the partial revolution, are to be deplored, but there's no going back to rule from the past when technical thought expects a cyber and computer realm, and religious thought expects the Second Coming.

Today, the future is so popular many wonder if the past has any relevance! (But does this make us too easily led?)

Jesus Was Hit By Total Backlash

Jesus was slain for his use of Christian power, but his subsequent overcoming of death opened the way for us.

Only he could have undergone death and emerged victorious, because he had an origin from on high.

Despite the uniqueness of his mission, he instructed his disciples and followers to take up the cross.

Did he mean undergo death as he did on the cross? No, because he did that one time for all. I believe he meant we must face the opposition, risk the blows, and continue to follow him along the road which only he could have unblocked for us.

He was hated, and said his followers would be hated.

Backlash Hit Disciples And Other Followers

The disciples were hated by the worldly powers because they were out there with ministries of overcoming.

They all met violent deaths, my mother often recited, puzzled why they weren't advanced enough to be protected. I don't know the answer, except that the particular, concentrated mental and physical opposition, so determined to overturn Jesus and his teachings, was more intense and complex than that coming against, for example, even such an ancient worthy as Daniel.

The disciples' preaching and converting exposed them to the major backlash of the times, which had to win or else abandon the field in defeat. Thus I believe this opposition was too great for them at the moment. Along the way, though, most had many remarkable instances of protection.

Not only the activist followers were persecuted. Mere professing Christians, many of whom weren't far up the "ladder," were eaten by lions in Roman spectacles held in front of great crowds in arenas.

Despite individual deaths and group slaughters, Early Christianity grew. We've all heard the expression that martyrs' blood was the "seed" of the church.

Backlash Soon Resulted In
Divine Healing Being Shoved Aside

As discussed in a previous chapter, Early Christianity's divine healing was gradually, then finally, excluded by what became the state church.

No higher power could be permitted than emperors and the empire, kings and kingdoms—or, for that matter, the developing new church's personages and systems.

Power-Christianity was a threat. The closed-type governmental structures of the day had to resist it or face modification at the least, overthrow at the most.

Ladder-Climbing In The End-Times Can't Be Overthrown, And Will Overthrow Evil

Evil, believed to be the ultimate power, still rules on earth. However, divine good will establish a new regime, "on earth, as it is in heaven." After the macro defeat of evil, the remainder, dethroned, will decline and eventually come to an end (Rev. 21:4).

Ladder-Climbing Separates Sheep From Goats

Do we get rid of bad people or do we rid bad people— including ourselves—of badness? The very word "healing" implies the correction of mortals.

The chaff separates from the wheat in us as we go up the ladder. It's a vigorous experience.

I believe there's a "sheep" and "goat" in each of us: the sheep the climber awakening to identity as an image and likeness of God, and the goat the conception of ourselves as material humans "born of a woman, and of few days and full of trouble."

Separating doesn't harm the human identity—a very important point—but helps it change and climb. (Nevertheless, our identities may undergo an ore-refining process as deep as that explained in Malachi 3:2-3.)

Personal tribulations don't mean that there won't be a biblically-prophesied, general period of tribulation.

(Today, instead of Bible-authorized separation on the tribulum or threshing board, the world is trying to homogenize evil and good—make everything acceptable.)

Some Taken, Some Left Behind?

Will the meeting "in the air" with Christ (I Thes. 4:17) remove people from earth? The Bible's message is the coming of the kingdom of God on earth. If there is not to be an interruption, then the verses cited simply relate to Christ's coming, and to our spiritual awakening to higher being. Those changed by the encounter join the ranks of Christians empowered to answer Jesus' call as "labourers" in the "harvest" (Mat. 9:36-38), overcoming evil on earth.

If two are "in the field," with one taken and the other left (Mat. 24:37, 40), I continue to believe this means each of us awakens to higher being. This is progress, but we can't just walk away from our mortal natures. It ain't that easy.

Enoch's ascension left no mortal remained because he had worked his way out of mortalhood. There was no more threshing to be done. In the latter days, those who get their first great awakening to higher status as in Ephesians 4:13, still have plenty of tribulation ahead.

"Self-immolation" is thought to obtain spiritual life by burning up the mortal. I can't see how religious suicide has any place in Christianity where Paul said sacrifice was by a "new" and "living" way. A Christian sense, it would seem to me, relates to beneficial tribulation (not destructive—a threshing not a trashing,) on the order of Malachi 3:2-3 whereby the lower identity is ministered to, not killed, abandoned, terminated, or lost.

Flames Of Holy Ghost Fire

The flames of Scriptural destruction are usually "Holy Ghost fire," not the flames of the fiery furnace from which God protects his children.

Our Depths Get Probed When We Climb

When climbing, the light we encounter exposes hidden things beneath our floorboards which usually we'd rather hide. A very important point is that divine light doesn't eradicate any part of our human identity, and shouldn't be used in a threatening way. Instead, it aids in the benevolent transformation of our "pits."

If we have false pride in our holiness, we can suddenly receive a shock when divine light gets down in our basement—and we can find we need divine grace as never before.

If the evils underneath are devils, they're cast out. However, if they're part of our tripartite human psyche, such as depths and shadows of the libido, or even splits or multiples, we cannot religiously murder but must heal. How can we tell the difference? Sometimes by spiritual sunshine ripening the wheat and the tares, other times by divine insights or words from God that give us a separation, or that dissolve the evil but never our sense of identity, even if it's the darkest and most hopeless on earth.

God doesn't kill the sinner any more than Jesus killed Mary Magdalene. Our sinful natures are replaced by the divine by degrees.

Just as with our own natures, if we've attacked or neglected to minister to the bottommost elements in other individuals and society, this will impede our progress.

Can One Slide Off The Ladder?

If a climber slides, this is just a form of backlash, a reversal, and one can overcome it and push forward.

The main sliding today isn't even on the ladder. It's the world's seemingly-exhilarating and penalty-free greased ride away from the ladder. The sensation is of climbing, but the participants will find themselves like the man who left Jerusalem.

Nonetheless, when the "crunch" phase comes for those people, there's no place they can be that God won't reach them (as Paul and David both said, Rom. 8:38 and Ps. 139:8-10) if they pray diligently to readapt and reconnect with the divine they've shut out.

No Passive Salvation

As we climb the ladder, the popular idea of a passive salvation trip to heaven yields to the biblical teachings, "work out your own salvation" (Paul in Phil. 2:12); and "faith without works is dead" (Jas. 2:17, 20, 26).

If we weren't engaged in overcoming, would we really be following Christ Jesus?

Divine grace saves us, but we don't receive much of it when we sit on our duffs. We have to work, and show God's works.

A climbing life is a working life, a proving life.

And part of that life is ministerial: an individual prayer ministry if not a pulpit or mission ministry.

-

*In the 1500s and 1600s, Collective Thought
Had To Battle For The Very Right To Climb,
Initiating The Breakout From "Night"*

Freedom and growth for thought, speech, religion, and scientific investigation and practice, were and are necessary to the ladder of progress and the Jacob-change "Israel. "

The Renaissance or "rebirth" began the long process of breakout from Jesus' prophesied period of "night." Many other steps and people ended both the "Dark Ages" (which technically ran only to about 1000) and the overlapping Middle Ages or Medieval period (from the fall of Rome in 476 to about 1500). Other steps and people continued the progress, which is accelerating today.

The science of Galileo (circa 1600) and others was bitterly resisted primarily because it challenged authority.

The Church of that time, interwoven with the secular rulers, held absolute positions on nearly everything.

Challenges to those positions went to the heart of the governing system. Thoughts religious and scientific that were out of line could bring one before the Inquisition where Galileo, for one, was forced to recant.

Luther's theses in 1517 rattled the grip the Church had on everything but didn't change its opposition to progress.

Printing made Bibles—actually, portions of them—available to the people. Prior to this, the Word emanated almost solely from clergy, who maintained tight control on biblical interpretation.

As soon as people could read and evaluate for themselves, and listen individually for the Holy Spirit, independent thought was aroused. Old religious concepts were challenged, and new denominations offered choices.

The Renaissance period, marked at its beginning by Da Vinci and Michaelangelo (1500 for a quick handle on dates), gave collective consciousness its first major crossing of mental, intellectual, and scientific frontiers since divine healing vanished in Jesus' prophesied "night."

The Church showed a little "give" when it accepted and used Renaissance art, sculpture and architecture (certainly a science). Despite progress, inquisitions remained.

Post-Renaissance Climbers Sought The "New Land"

After the various breakouts, people again sought the Promised Land, New Jerusalem, New Canaan, and so on.

Exploration and *discovery* (concepts formerly blocked) widely breached the once-fortified walls of harshly-imposed old thought, while consciousness expanded.

Certainly, Spiritual Ladder-Climbers Produced The New American Nation

In the founding of the US, great words proclaiming rights and freedoms were stated by a *government* for the first time in history.

US progress was ordained and specially empowered.

God doesn't say, "You're going to have wars and expand bloodily over the continent." God knows His own Realm right here, and we undergo changes as we seek it.

The expansion was inevitable, but the bloody part was not God-ordained. In the case of the Indians, many had a higher sense of the Great Spirit than did their conquerors.

Does God ignore our plight? Or do we ignore God's Kingdom where we can obtain our solutions?

The ladder, appearing in our thought, points toward comprehending the higher reality which dissolves evil.

When we enter God's knowing, the problems which seemed so real in our consciousness dissolve.

God's Kingdom, sought and partly found in prayer, will continue to produce a Jacob-change, "Israel" America.

This will soon accelerate.

A spiritually powerful, climbing America is what this nation stands for in the world picture. It will be drastically challenged from inside and outside, but grow as the result.

To blend the US with the rest of the world is to mistake our mission.

Our mission is certain to be accomplished, despite the present national mental and physical pollution which runs counter to it.

Are all Americans part of the "Israel change" population? No more than all early Hebrews were.

The US—A Great Place For Ladder Climbers

When Jefferson wrote that "all men are created equal," he certainly wasn't recognizing the state of humans then or now, even "under the law."

In my opinion, he glimpsed something of "man in the image and likeness of God" as spoken of in the first chapter of Genesis. (The second chapter tells us of our ever-popular material man, who was in trouble from the start.)

A lyricist was later to write of our beloved US, "Thine alabaster cities gleam, undimmed by human tears...." We have no such places, and never have had them.

Instead, didn't that composer glimpse something of the higher Realm that is so pervasive and inevitable on our soil?

"God shed his grace on thee." America has been immeasurably blessed and protected.

The inspirations I've received in the US West have topped anything in world travels. It isn't mountain peaks and beautiful scenes by themselves that inspire, but the degree of spiritual seeing, which seems to be easier in our country.

To the degree that the US attempts to homogenize with the rest of the world (and, like Samson, chooses baser things, and refuses higher things) it will come into a testing time. This cannot be avoided.

Directly ahead, the secular aspect of the US and of nations around the world will become even more intense.

Irregardless, the divine difference in the US will steadily emerge.

Part of the US collective consciousness is spiritual and attuned to the divine. This isn't just in the sense of "see you in the hereafter," but in the right-now sense of realizing a higher reality that changes us and the nation.

This makes the US a great place for ladder climbing.

< >

5
THE POWER NEEDED TO WIN: SINGLE, DOUBLE, AND FINAL

To Win, We'll Have To Become Overcomers
Using The Powers Described In Scripture

"To him that overcometh will I grant to sit with me in my throne, even as I also overcame, and am set down with my Father in his throne" (Rev. 3:21).

How do we overcome? Levels of power are mentioned, leading to Revelation's prophecy: "And there shall be no more death, neither sorrow, nor crying, neither shall there be any more pain: for the former things are passed away" (Rev. 21:4).

Elisha Had Single Power, But
Sought And Got Double Power

Elisha studied under the great prophet Elijah (Elias), and aspired to the same level of power his master possessed.

When Elisha learned his teacher would ascend, he asked to receive a "double portion" of his spirit.

To this request, Elijah gave a strange answer, saying that if his student *saw* him ascending, he would then *have* the "double" power.

That is, if Elisha could see beyond human limitations into the divine realm where Elijah was going, this would indicate a very advanced stage of Elisha's thought—one where he would possess the double power.

Elisha watched his master ascend, and became a renowned healer and prophet after that.

He had possessed a certain level of power, but knew there was more. Since he asked for double, I'll call his original level of power single.

In biblical ascension one transforms out, leaving no remains. This implies understanding of higher being.

Did others in the Bible besides Elijah ascend? Yes, Jesus, of course. Also Enoch, before the Flood. And personally I believe Moses also ascended, because his body was never found, and he appeared with Elijah before Jesus on the Mount of Transfiguration.

What's the difference between the two levels of power? Is "double" just a stepping-up of "single"? No.

In "single," the basic concept is the mortal condition, and divinity is prayed for, or applied, with beneficial results.

In double power, the mortal realizes divine identity— an entirely different, higher reality—and works from that far more authoritative and certain standpoint.

Between the two, there's plenty of overlap and going back and forth.

Jesus Referred To Both Levels
In His Instructions To Followers

Jesus said, "He that believeth on me, the works that I do shall he do also; and greater works than these shall he do" (Jn. 14:12). Thus he referred to two levels of power—a regular level, one might say, and "greater."

Most people are not engaged even in the exercise of "single" power in divine healing works. That first step is coming rapidly. Soon, millions will practice divine healing in the manner of Jesus' inner and wider circles of disciples where the power was about halfway between single and greater.

When Jesus said we would do "greater" works, did he mean more remarkable works? No, because his greatest work was overcoming death—opening the door for all of us—and it's hard to see how anyone could do something more important than that.

Therefore, I believe "greater" meant works from the greater standpoint where he lived his life.

Jesus' disciples watched his Ascension, but unlike Elisha at Elijah's ascension, they didn't get double power then because they didn't fully perceive what was going on—their vision obscured by a "cloud" (Acts 1:9).

Christians generally accept that Jesus was a higher identity, temporarily appearing in a fleshly form. Peter declared to him, "Thou art the Christ, the son of the living God." Confirming this, Jesus added that "flesh and blood" had not revealed it unto Peter, but God (Mat. 16:13-18).

For us to get the double power, we'll have to see him in his higher form—comprehend his present state.

It's not difficult for us to believe that Jesus, the higher being, could work wonders.

It's difficult, though, to believe that *we* could do such things, as he said we would. Of course, that requires change.

What Special Element Appears
In The "Greater" Or "Double" Level?

A divine identity is the special element. Not the human spirit, but a wholly spiritual identity in the image of God for each of us.

John wrote, "It doth not yet appear what we shall be: but...when he shall appear, we shall be like him; for we shall see him as he is" (I Jn. 3:2). John had seen Jesus, yet knew that "as he is" was a different state.

He also said that when we saw him, we would have a being "like him."

Speaking of this higher status, John said elsewhere, "As many as received him, to them gave he power to become the sons of God...." (Jn. 1:12).

In this line, Paul later wrote, "We know that if our earthly house of this tabernacle were dissolved, we have a... house not made with hands, eternal in the heavens" (II Cor. 5:1). His next verses continue this theme of divine identity available to us.

Paul also wrote, "We all, with open face beholding... the glory of the Lord, are changed into the same image from glory to glory...." (II Cor. 3:18).

As the genuine concept progressively appears, it is prophesied that many will claim they are Christ (Mat. 24: 24). Others will claim their personal, human "I" is the divine identity. However, these things are only the serpent-proclaimed "as gods" state (Gen. 3:5) not divine revelation.

Jesus' Predictions For Greater Power
Were For Latter Christianity

The Early Christian Fellowship had the single power, and had touched the hem of the double. Jesus predicted "night" for the early power-Christianity, when no man could "work the works of him that sent me" (Jn. 9:4).

He predicted the Holy Ghost would "bring all things to your remembrance, whatsoever I have said unto you" (Jn. 14:26). These predictions logically relate to the renewal of divine healing power, and to the Second Coming period and activity, and to the overcoming of all evil in the latter days.

Seeing Jesus in his ascended state as in I Thessalonians 4:17 is certainly part of the Second Coming, and this viewing is also what produces double power as we grasp a tiny bit of what John meant when he said, "we shall be like him."

Consider, in all this, that Jesus said, "Lo, I am with you alway" (Mat. 28:20).

Old Testament Appearances

The Bible tells us of the Christ-identity presence long before the birth of Jesus in a fleshly state.

Paul, writing of the Exodus, said they did "all drink

the same spiritual drink: for they drank of that spiritual Rock that followed them: and that Rock was Christ" (I Cor. 10:4).

Paul explained Jesus had a spiritual, eternal status able to be perceived on the Exodus, and a fleshly, temporal one. He wrote, "Who, being in the form of God, thought it not robbery to be equal with God: But made himself of no reputation, and took upon him the form of a servant, and was made in the likeness of men" (Phil 2:6-7).

Jesus himself spoke of his Old Testament contact with David, saying that David made reference to his *presence* at that time (1,000 years earlier).

Regarding that, Jesus asked those around him, "What think ye of Christ? whose son is he? They say unto him, The Son of David. He saith unto them, How then doth David in spirit call him Lord...?" (Mat. 41-45).

Clearly, the Christ-identity is above fleshly man.

Then Shouldn't We Be Looking For Him In His Higher State?

Many now seek in that direction, under the prophecy of "meeting him in the air" (I Thes. 4:17).

Instead Of Waiting For Heaven To Act, Don't We Have To Act?

Don't we have to accept what he said: that he is with us "alway," climb, meet him "as he is," learn a little of our spiritual identity, be changed, and gain power to overcome?

Overcomers

Overcomers are mentioned in various ways in Revelation—for example, in chapters 2 and 3:

"To him that overcometh will I give to eat of the tree of life" (Rev. 2:7).

"He that overcometh shall not be hurt of the second death" (2:11).

"To him that overcometh will I give to eat of the hidden manna, and...a new name written, which no man knoweth, save he that receiveth it" (2:17).

"He that overcometh and keepeth my works unto the end, to him will I give power over the nations" (2:26).

"He that overcometh, the same shall be clothed in white raiment..." (Rev. 3:5).

"Him that overcometh will I make a pillar in the temple of my God...and I will write upon him my new name" (3:12).

"To him that overcometh will I grant to sit with me in my throne, even as I also overcame, and am set down with my Father in his throne" (Rev. 3:21).

The Trend Line
Of The Book Revelation:
The End Of All Evil

The end-time struggles and victories lead to this: "And God shall wipe away all tears from their eyes; and there shall be no more death, neither sorrow, nor crying, neither shall there be any more pain: for the former things are passed away" (Rev. 21:4).

For "Harvest" Workers,
Jesus Asked

Referring to the "harvest," Jesus asked for "labourers" (Mat. 9:36-38). The sense of the text is fruition—the successful completion of spiritual efforts.

It Takes The Early And Latter Rain
To Produce Harvest

The Bible refers to the "former" or "early" rains, and the "latter" rains, in a very spiritual sense.

In Joel we read, "Be glad then, ye children of Zion, and rejoice in the Lord your God: for he...will cause to come down for you the rain, the former rain, and the latter rain in the first month. And the floors shall be full of wheat, and the fats [vats] shall overflow with wine and oil. And I will restore to you the years that the locust hath eaten.... (Joel 2:23-25).

This prophetic sense is also found in Hosea. "Then shall we know, if we...know the Lord: his going forth is prepared as the morning; and he shall come to us as the rain, as the latter rain and former rain unto the earth" (Hos. 6:3).

The statement in Joel, "And I will restore to you the years the locust hath eaten" unmistakably refers to a higher revelation. How else could the past be restored or even compensated for in the present, unless the divine kingdom was being revealed, which was never touched by loss or death?

In what would appear to cover both early and latter,

Jesus promised a revelation of "all things...whatsoever I have said unto you" (Jn. 14:26)—everything he tried to teach us but our "dull" ears and "closed" eyes (Mat. 13:15) didn't comprehend.

The Two Bible Witnesses Represent Early And Latter Power-Christianity And Other Things

In Revelation, we read about the "two witnesses" (11: 3-12). They are the two candlesticks and olive trees (Rev. 11:3-4), and olive trees and branches (Zech. 4:3, 11-14).

They represent the two essentials: Jesus' spiritual identity and the explanation, which very much includes us, and enables us to get out.

They represent the first and second comings. In the first, he came to us, in the second, we find him "as he is," and to be always present.

They represent early and latter power-Christianity.

The early and latter don't strictly represent single and double power respectively, but the latter particularly relates to the double power coming on earth in a broad and unstoppable way.

Due to the ladder or steps whereby we gain spirituality and change, can we skip the early and just practice the latter? No, it's logical that the early would come first, or have to be filled in later before the latter could progress. We don't have to return in time, but can experience the early in its present, resurrected forms, including spiritual encounters, the gifts, and the changes which the early produces in us.

We'll be learning a lot more about both early and latter in the years ahead, as it takes both to produce harvest.

Preaching Together—In Sackcloth

The Bible says the two witnesses preach together in the last days clothed in sackcloth (which denotes repentance).

Why the sackcloth? I think it's because the early and latter ignored or tossed brickbats at one another before they realized they were on the same team, practicing Christian healing, although maybe at different rungs of the ladder.

Preaching Together, The Followers Draw Double Backlash

Preaching together, the two witnesses represent the potential for harvest, therefore evil *has* to strike back with all it can muster.

This double opposition holds nothing in reserve because it's *do or die* for evil. It has to try to kill the two witnesses.

The Bible says the "beast" kills them (Rev. 11:7).

Their Dead Bodies

"Their dead bodies" lie in the "street of the great city, which spiritually is called Sodom and Egypt, where also our Lord was crucified" (Rev. 11:8).

They Resurrect, Then Ascend

Their resurrection shocks the detractors who were jubilant at their demise. Then they *ascend* (Rev. 11: 11-12).

One—No Longer Two

The two concepts become one, a new form.

Unified Followers Are Set To Win

Jesus overcame death first. Now the unified followers have overcome the worst that evil could throw at them.

Possessing now the final power which comes at this stage, the overcomers are set for the defeat of evil on earth.

Revelation Chapter 12— The Devil Tossed From "Heaven"

"And the great dragon was cast out, that old serpent, called the Devil, and Satan, which deceiveth the whole world...." (Rev. 12:9).

Humans have believed the "dragon" was in heaven, or at the least had cosmic powers of sorts, or had some relationship to Deity ranging from outright adversarial to mutual accommodation. Some have believed evil and good to be simply two sides of Deity.

Actually, evil has nothing to do with the all-good God —and therein lies the ability to destroy it.

Devil A Liar And A Lie

Jesus called him a "liar" and proved him a lie.
The dragon was not only deceiving us, but a deception.

It's cast from our concept of heaven, and now we're able to really get to work.

The entire presentation of a power apart from say, the high God of the 23rd Psalm, is a lie.

Evil has no reality beyond what it can deceive us into believing. (Admittedly, this amount of deception is prodigious!)

Does God Kill? Or Is Killing Instead In The Realm Of The Carnal Mind?

Traditionally, humans have believed the highest authority included the power to kill. Many believe God will someday lose His patience and destroy the devil, simultaneously eradicating up to billions of sinners.

A Mental Gymnastic

Is the ability to deliver negative force as the ultimate power, "good"? Can we worship such a power with *all* our "heart, soul, mind and strength"—and not have great mental reservations plus compartments?

An unpredictable Deity who doesn't practice what He commands ("Thou shalt not kill") presents a dichotomy.

Besides, how do we overcome evil if God is using it—or has it in His arsenal and might use it?

How do we overcome evil if God isn't totally with us?

In the purification of the end-time, the high God of, say, the 23rd Psalm, will be worshiped more and more.

When "Cast Out Into The Earth" (Rev. 12:9)
The Devil Creates Big Problems

"Woe to the inhabiters of the earth and of the sea! for the devil is come down unto you, having great wrath, because he knoweth that he hath but a short time" (Rev. 12:12).

Tossed Out By The "Blood Of The Lamb"
And By The "Word Of Their Testimony"—
That Is, By The Combination Of Early And Latter

"They overcame him by the blood of the Lamb and by the word of their testimony" (Rev. 12:11). The "blood of the Lamb" is the early and "the word of their testimony" the latter (which includes, Jesus said, all of his teachings).

Evil In Its Death-throes
Wants To Kill Everything

Once the dragon sees it's losing, it will try to destroy the world and all people, even those still siding with it.

The dragon stands for death, and this will be its final assertion—attempted destruction of everything and itself.

In its best "liar" manner, it will continue to try to pin all this ill-will and killing on God.

Those who know their spiritual identities—whose "names are written in the book of life"—will present the divine indestructibility of person and place in the face of the preliminary and final throes of the dragon.

Great Struggles

Ensuing chapters in Revelation tell of great struggles in earth leading to various climaxes.

(For those tackling the Book of Revelation, do I think it's laid out in chronological order? No. In my opinion, whereas the framework certainly contains a general chronology, the many insights often overlap as they reach back into history and forward into the enlightened future.)

The Devil Into The Pit

The defeated devil is thrown into the "pit" for a thousand years.

In that battle, "Faithful and True" comes as a warrior on a white horse, with a "name written, that no man knew, but he himself" (Rev. 19:11-12). "He was clothed with a vesture dipped in blood: and his name is called The Word of God" (v. 13).

(Note that again we have the blood and the Word. And combined. And victorious.)

The name, "Word of God," and also the concept of a name written which no man knew but himself, would certainly appear to depict Christ Jesus in a high form of his divine identity, not limited by mortal man's stereotypes and above what our mortal names could name, or minds grasp.

And "the armies which were in heaven followed him" (v. 14). The unified, resurrected, victorious followers are with him.

Although At This Point The Tables Are Turned
Permanently, The Job Is Still Not Complete

At this point (which I call the macro defeat of evil), divine power has the upper hand—and *on earth,* not just in heaven. Evil will never again have the upper hand.

However, evil will still be a problem for a time because the job on earth *worldwide* will not yet be *finished.*

Billions will have to get busy on the course symbolized by the Exodus, and all the other significant steps taken later.

Then—No More Death

The holy city comes down (appears), and "there shall be no more death, neither sorrow, nor crying, neither shall there be any more pain" (Rev. 21:4-7).

Those same passages also remind us, "He that overcometh shall inherit all things; and I will be his God, and he shall be my son."

So our army of warriors will indeed be right in the middle of the action all the way to the final end of evil.

< >

6
THE FIRST EMPIRE CONCEPT TO RECKON WITH: EGYPT

Ancient Empires In The End-Time?
First, Some Background

Will the six Bible empires rise singly or as part of the seventh empire "not yet come," to fight to the death the coming Kingdom of God on earth? Some interpreters think so.

The ancients fell, but their many special evils such as Rome's spirit of world conquest didn't die. Thus it's logical that these evils could join forces in one final empire to oppose God.

Revelation tells us of "seven kings: five are fallen, and one is, and the other is not yet come" (17:10). The five fallen were Egypt, Assyria, Babylon, Medio-Persia, and Greece. The one existing was Rome. That leaves one "not yet come." Regarding that, Revelation mentions "666," apparently the ruler of the final, seventh, and one-world empire.

Five of the six oldies conquered and occupied Canaan, while Egypt earlier enslaved the Hebrews.

The Advanced Empire Of "666"

The final empire will be a quantum jump above the ancients. The leader may appear religious, charming and traditional, but will be "tomorrow," scientific and cunning.

The ancient evils, by unifying under one authority, will seek an advanced level of end-time power to offset the Christian overcomers unifying and obtaining power).

Will some of the physical empires actually rise under the umbrella of the final bad empire? Probably. Persia (Iran), Babylon (Iraq), and Assyria (northern Iraq and Iran) are situated in one oil-soaked region from whence they can help control the world, and are hostile to Israel and the US.

Will There Be One Giant Battle Or Several Climaxes Over A Period Of Time?

The latter, as the coming of the divine kingdom, already beyond dawn into the early morning, progresses. Evil, restless, is emerging from hiding, becoming bolder, struggling mentally and physically, and oozing seductions.

What Were The Central Essences Of The Oldies— Empire By Empire, Starting With Egypt?

In this and the next chapters, we'll take up the old empires one by one, comment on their evils still existent in the present, and speculate on the VIIth empire, "not yet come."

-

I
Egypt

The Pyramid; Also Oppression
Of The Hebrews; And Mammon

(None of the below is directed at today's nation or people. We're talking about the biblically symbolic "Egypt.")

What's the big deal about a pyramid?
Is the great pyramid-tomb of Giza dangerous?
No, but the form and its monumental stone statement symbolizes the biblical carnal mind's organizational structure imposed historically for governments, corporations, the military, families, tennis tournaments, and condo associations! And if "666" is to rule the world in opposition to God's kingdom coming on earth, this has to be from the top of a pyramid.

The pyramid is a "rule-from-the-top" structure. Its ever-narrowing form as it goes up creates constant strife as fewer and fewer positions have to be fought over, bringing out the very worst both in those climbing and those gripping the limited seats at any level. It *requires* a large bottom.

Contrast The Pyramid To The
"City Foursquare" Divine Form

Pyramid admirers like to say that *anyone* can reach the top; however, it's plain that *every*one can't.
This is in contrast to the coming Kingdom's "city foursquare" (Rev. 21) which has no layers to battle over.

In the pyramid, do those who work the hardest get to the top? Nah—the hardest workers are rowing in the galleys.

But surely, skill and talent will get you to the top, right? That's true for a few (as well as for a few hard workers), but the trails are littered with the bones of skilled, talented, and hardworking people kept down, robbed, disappointed, or shoved out.

For every skilled, talented, or hardworking person at the pyramid top, there've been a dozen who were just lucky, or connivers, militarists, murderers, thieves of the money or reputation of others, inheritors, charmers with good looks or sex appeal, the "destined," plain dodos, and so on.

In big corporations, many have risen so mystically that they wonder, "What am I doing here?" and, "Do I deserve this?" Norman Vincent Peale wrote of this because so many sought his counsel on these points.

Many rise simply because the pyramid mind—the Bible's carnal mind—has positions to fill, especially in today's expansion from local to global, from scattered to consolidated. And many fall for the same reason.

Some seem "born" to rise to the top or to run things, while others fight it out exhibiting Genghis Khan-like qualities, or the slipperiest of craftiness, in order to gain control of even little corners of not-important levels.

Pyramid Requires One's Soul

Whether one climbs with spurs or is wafted up by luck, sooner or later one must sell one's soul, or increments thereof. In God, though, one finds identity and a way of life.

Pyramid A "Food Chain"

At its mildest, the pyramid is a "pecking order."
Always, it's an elimination tournament.
At its worst, it's an outright "food chain."

Despite glamor, even the top ain't safe. Monarchs have been stabbed and poisoned, young heirs bagged and taken into the deep woods. Yesterday's sports and entertainment heroes vanish from the spotlight as shining replacements move up.

Pyramid Diminishes The Individual

The pyramid in Western Culture today glorifies a few at the top in a way that diminishes the majority. Instead of seeking their own spiritual identity and status, the crowds are busy reestablishing gods, royalty, nobility and similar forms from which we originally fled. By identifying with the top figures in sports, money, and entertainment (and even with products), identity and status are gained even if one is well down in the pile.

What's really needed is individual development in democracy and religion—things the US was founded upon.

Down At The Hopeless Levels,
Once There Were Revolutions

Revolutions once occurred amongst the masses envious of the top and fearing they were blocked out forever.

This pressure has been recently alleviated by huge lotteries. Every day someone wins a fortune putting him or her in the financial upper class. So there's "hope" which keeps the peasants from boiling over, even while they transfer their money via dead tickets to the lucky few.

The saddest thing about lotteries is that every "winner" stands on the bones of countless losers.

Worse for all participants: as they embrace good luck, they take in all that bad luck which is an intrinsic part of it.

Too, in lotteries, nothing is created or discovered. One has just surrendered to the pyramidal chance-life system.

Pyramid Democratic Or Autocratic?

Is the pyramid essentially democratic or autocratic? It sure ain't democratic.

Much of the most acrimonious fighting between political parties or voters in the US has been between those wanting a corporate-pyramid framework within our governmental system, and those who favor the mass.

The US corporate money top once was not trusted, and was treated with caution even when liked. Today, all this has done a caution-to-the-winds "180."

Traditionally, democracies have tempered unrestrained pyramids, but today *corpocracy has tempered democracy.*

"Pyramid Science": Amalgamation Until There's Just One Remaining

In the "science of the pyramid," the most dangerous element is the pyramid's need and destiny to amalgamate.

In a wiser past, when we were frightened of empires and business monopolies, we restricted the raw pyramid.

But times have changed. Now we love the pyramids and vicariously identify with their main figures and products. We've become a "fan class" displaying advertising logos on our clothes. We no longer ask the age-old questions "Who am I?" and "Why am I here?" Our cosmic realm where we look for deep answers is cyberspace.

"666" Pyramid Coming?

The biggest pyramid of all time is the prophesied world government of "666" (Rev. 13). Since it's to be ruled by one "man," it's obvious that this is control from the top, and can only be done from the peak of a pyramid.

The ruler requires a mark in the hand or in the forehead in order to "buy or sell."

This sounds like a commercial pyramid.

How will it come to power? By tanks and artillery like Hitler? I think instead it will silently form a governmental layer *above* traditional governments, leaving them to function more or less as before but in a reduced status, and not in control of international commerce and finance.

I believe this is already partly installed.

Corporations are presently consolidating, or merging, at an unprecedented rate worldwide. Stock buyers become excited because there's more than just a hint that part ownership of the giants is part ownership of the world— certainly of the controlling "top."

There's increasing speculation about who or what "666" may be.

My favorite analysis is my own: 666 is a symbol for the corporate legal entity—considered by law to be a person.

Today we see "group monopolies. "

Once, the US trembled at mere single-field national monopolies (the "trusts" like oil and banks). But today, a relatively few buddy-buddy international conglomerates effectively rule commerce worldwide, and we aren't alarmed.

Individually in some cases, and certainly collectively, these firms are already larger than nations—larger even than some blocs of nations. They exercise much more influence and control in national legislatures, parliaments, monarchies, juntas, and other relics, than you do—you outdated voter, you.

I smile as I say that, but it's no longer a confident smile.

A Pyramidal World Commercial "Supra" Or "Over" Government Is Already Strong

International commercial and financial interests are already operating as a worldwide "supra" government above the heads of nations.

The US is taking the lead in allowing this.

This isn't a "*super*-government" like a dictatorship or a consolidation of governments, but a "*supra*" one leaving governments in place below while riding above as "international commerce and finance" which nations can't govern (but which progressively govern today's global nations).

I Call It The Global "Overzone" Or "Suprazone"

Global group monopolies dominate world extraction, manufacture, transportation, finance, and distribution. They are deeply woven into governments, which are at their feet.

It's been a slow upcreep and increep, often enticing.

We must wake up to the fact of this new upper zone and its makeup—and that it is *not controllable by voters or mere nations* singly or in blocs.

I call it the "overzone"—the new stratum above nations. The global "suprazone."

"Short" Democracy

When an "overzone" comes into place above an existing and proven democracy such as the US, it doesn't have to change the form of government.

Instead, what happens as we "go global" is that our national government stays in place as before; however, our voters have little or no say over global commerce or finance, or the corporations or group monopolies thereof, riding above us and heavily influencing us.

This is what I call "short" democracy.

To exaggerate a point, we can still elect dogcatchers.

Democracy here and elsewhere is getting shorter as even *domestic* affairs at the top are less controllable than before, and global affairs of the "supratop" are uncontrollable.

Even if our people beheld the "suprazone" and its perils, they wouldn't know what to do about it, because the issues don't appear on ballots, and candidates don't campaign on those issues.

Democracy is said to be sweeping the world, but often the newer democracies have but limited constitutions riddled with loopholes for the old-style powers, while the people's capabilities are not great. Also, the "supra" is usually solidly in place, often with inside cooperation.

There's no hole in this "overzone" layer. It's getting more influential, more governmental.

Is Less Government Always Less Government?

Although I support the general idea of less government, what must be watched is whether a particular retreat by government is promoted mainly so the corpocracy—government by corporations—can move into the vacuum.

We see laws passed, laws changed, and also actions *not* taken in order to favor companies, when sometimes these things weaken the mass voter who's already on the ropes.

The Pyramid's Supposed Mystiques, Mysteries, And "Whatzit"

Some executives keep a crystal pyramid on their desk, wanting to receive or identify with its special energies or whatever.

We've all at some time wondered about the mysteries of the pyramid. Concerning the great one at Giza, scholarly books include charts outlining prophecy for the remainder of time, the "hidden" data "discovered" in the measurements of the hallways, and so on.

Many believe we know only a fraction of the pyramid-power secrets once known to Egyptians.

Are these supposed secrets buried deep inside the Egyptian mind? Or did the special knowledge perhaps go up in smoke when the library at Alexandria burned, losing forever the core wisdom of soothsayers and astrologers—literally the fundamentals of the universe?

I don't hold with any of that.

The "whatzit" of the pyramid mainly includes its ability to throw us into competitive frenzies—sometimes murderous, sometimes only where we love knocking off that team from across the country, or proving we're more suited for the vice-presidency of the company than that twerp from finance who never sold an account in the field.

The "whatzit" of the pyramid implies power by the top, and a control system throughout. Superiorism is involved in all aspects of the pyramid.

We "climb" socially or corporately—leave others behind, rise above.

Comparisons are constantly made to others, or others are denigrated to put them in a lower classification.

Today's Huge Corporate Pyramids Have Many New Mainly Control Layers

A publicly-traded company, when swimming in the unlimited capital of the world's financial markets, can amalgamate or consolidate again...and again...adding layer upon layer of corporate control *far above mere work* (and for that matter far above extraction, processing, manufacturing, selling and distribution).

The executive presently ruling an empire of many companies (or the brands which are the only things remaining of many companies), is removed from gut-level, shop-floor, work and other basic activity. He or she is mainly at a control level and out of touch with what was once at least two-thirds of the corporate picture: the worker.

The workers are located more and more in remote lands under remote contractors.

And the executive asks, "What can we take over next?"

More About Pyramid Science:
"Above The Law;
Divine Rights; "Gods"

The top in history, while often impure, even criminal, has usually appeared shining, sometimes as "gods," and "above the law."

The fabled King Henry VIII routinely drummed up cases against his wives and murdered them—legally and righteously, of course. And he was the head of the Church.

"Papa Joe" Stalin was a mass murderer on a scale comparable to Hitler—and was our ally. We didn't look under the tarp to see if the truck was full of bodies until well after the war, although certainly our leaders knew the score.

The top—being the top—is supposed to make the laws, but not necessarily abide by them.

Kings claimed their "divine right"—one of history's most abused concepts.

Democracies are supposed to know the divine right is with the people. But despite this, the US is rampantly trying to reestablish an economically royal class it once spent decades in this century getting off its back; and is continuing to set up its entertainment and sports royalty.

All along, the US has seemed to love the atmosphere of royalty—especially the tamed types such as found in Great Britain.

Roman emperors rose into a sort of "god space" higher than merely being the ruler and having divine rights.

The "god" concept in Rome mixed the human condition in the top with mythological divinity just above the top.

Egyptian pyramids were clad in white limestone so the top would commune with the sun god, Ra, by reflecting its rays—a sign of unification with earth...via the top.

All "royalty" is part of the framework of superiors who are believed to be closer to deific or cosmic powers than the grungy peasants (who, we should note here, were the beneficiaries of most of Jesus' ministry).

The serpent in Genesis promised that man would be "as gods" instead of as images and likenesses of God, the divine promise also stated in Genesis.

This serpent-predicted "as gods" man or woman is fighting against God; and I expect we'll see a lot more of this type of identity, and much more intensity, as things draw closer to the predicted climaxes. Revelation's "666" will probably be the world's worst example.

Closed-Top Pyramid Despots

One variety of pyramid has a closed top, indicating it's not reaching upward for divinity either real or mythological but is interested only in making the despotic power figure the lone ruler. Genghis Khan. Adolf.

Hitler demanded and got total loyalty from both his inner circle and people—and they stuck with "der Fuehrer" until Gotterdamerung. No one has been able to figure that out yet, but I suspect we'll see more of that sort of thing before it's all over.

In many cases throughout history, such rulers existed

more inside their palace courts than outside. Examples were Marie Antoinette, the Czars, and the Shah of Iran. They were deluded; the pipple weren't behind them.

-

The Pyramid's "Blame" System

"Round up the usual suspects." And let's get our asses out of here, Bogie and Claude.

One of the infamous mechanisms of the human mind is to accuse someone else.

Even the little three-year-old kid ripping one in the movie theater turned to his Mom (the newspaper account read) and loudly said, "Excuse *you,* Mommie"—to the amusement of the house.

Hitler had to have his Jewish targets on whom to blame everything—to the point of trying to justify their extermination by falsely charging blameworthiness, and saying that things would be better and cleaner after the Jews were gone.

The blame system began with the carnal mind blaming its creation for the carnal mind's own failings, then placing everyone under the sentence of death for things not primarily their fault. And all under this mind die (see Rom. 8:6).

Jesus overturned that, but we're yet to realize it, follow him, and overcome the "last enemy" as he overcame it first.

Traditionally, the spike of death hangs over us while its accusations of blame for sins ("sins" that sometimes are simply normal living), jab at us.

Experiencing the finger of accusation, people often divert it to someone else.

Or occasionally they become a type of "holy" preacher who spends most of the time blaming others in "God's" name.

In the pyramid, the "blame negs"—both specific and nonspecific— constantly travel downward.

Those underneath who can dump them off onto others might rise a bit, being lighter.

Those who can't get rid of them, or at least stay even, load up and sink.

Unfortunates in the bottom areas are awash in a sea of negatives secular and religious, hidden and overt, subliminal and conscious—including judgments, oppressions, scorns, unfair characterizations, exclusions, twistings, superiorisms inflicted on presumed inferiors, defeats, and expressions of disgust and reproach. Through it all there's a type of mental presumption that rape of another's consciousness or even the physical killing of others is less blameworthy, or is even righteous, if delivered by the top.

Certain types of parasite bugs such as fleas need "blood hosts" to live on. Downward-trending negatives aren't much different. They all need "living hosts" ("grounds" might be another word, as if for electrical discharges) to absorb them.

Worthy Of Blame If Merely
Located In The Pyramid Bottom

The bottom people are often presumed to somehow be morally to blame because they're there.

The slave drivers of history frequently were respected members of the system—righteous, even churchgoing—while slaves were characterized as thieves and rogues, and were often the first to be accused and convicted in unsolved criminal cases.

"All colored people steal," the 1800s Dixie plantation whites might have told you, while overlooking the fact that their society stole the slaves' bodies, freedom, property, rights, futures, and so on.

The French Army once actually settled some of its unsolved criminal cases by choosing by lot an unfortunate from its lowest ranks to be sent up or shot. Kirk Douglas appeared in a movie about this.

Police, while showing their best side to the respected top, can display harsh negatives towards the bottom.

White collar is treated differently from the rest of the pyramid. The upper regions make the rules, pay the police, socialize with the judges. "White collar"—which extends well down into the pyramid—is treated as if "theirs didn't stink," and their crimes are lightly penalized while lower levels get the chains and the lash.

What? You Say The Pyramid Needs *The Bottom—*
And Creates And Maintains It
Because It Serves A Purpose?

Yes, and we overlook this in our societal reasoning.

Most of the talk about raising the bottom is mainly for political effect, and draws only token efforts.

However, we do offer the bottom a degree of minimum maintenance.

Why the necessity of the bottom? As mentioned, the pyramid must dispose of its psychic wastes.

The uppers must have lowers; the winners, losers; superiors, inferiors; the scornful, scornees; the falsely righteous, sinners; the we, them; the exclusive, someone to exclude; the rejecters, rejectees; and so on.

To dump is to cleanse. The top appears purer and higher by constant dumping, and the resultant pyramid peak shines enticingly because it's at an elevation where none can dump on it.

The middle—dumping about as much as it receives— remains mediocre.

The bottom gets twice as much negative force as it can dump off, and has no place to dump it.

Sometimes, one coming to help the bottom gets trashed, and asks, "Why?" The answer is that the people in the bottom need a place to dump.

The Bottom Should Try Rising?

If those in the bottom areas—physical or psychological—thought they saw negatives in the past, wait until they try to *rise* in the pyramid.

Those on the ever-narrowing levels above feel that any who are coming up are dangerous and likely to displace them. Reactions can range from strenuous to homicidal. However, love is sometimes extended by the top if a lower stratum stays down.

Movement is easier in times of pyramid expansion when those above don't feel threatened if a few more come up. Or in times of war, when there's a need. Or in times of the destruction of the particular pyramidal order, with a new one coming into place.

Contrariwise, in "crunch" times, movement upward for any stigmatized lower strata (in contrast to "upwardly mobile" activity among the accepted ones) can be harshly resisted, even reversed.

There's no denying that some who rise have a "charmed life," or talents welcomed by those above them.

Spiritual climbing, of course, is always available.

Churches have worthy charities, and I heartily support those as well as other private and also governmental activities to help the bottom. Nevertheless, there are few poor in the pews.

Worldwide, the bottom is growing incredibly. Even in the advanced, industrial nations, it still exists.

Some colonial church meetings had the "community" concept, with everyone there. The top families sat in their boxes with high sides like enclaves, the ordinary decent folks squeezed onto pews, and the sinners occupied a sinners' box in the rear. The servants had space in the rear or on the side, the slaves a place in the rear, side or balcony. The community's entire stratification was on display right there in the church.

Since then, though, the various church pyramids have long ago separated the classes by great distances, and issued twenty-foot poles to the uppers for fending off those they don't want to touch with ten-foot poles.

More Pyramid Science In Action—
The Scapegoat Theory

Study the scapegoat theories in, for example, *The Golden Bough*. The patterns are the same throughout time: The tribe gathers around the campfire; the sins (which the gods are imputing—or else why would the volcano be knocking everyone on their ashes?) have to be dealt with; therefore the goat is saddled with objects or pieces of cloth or whatever to represent the sins of the population; and finally the critter is driven from the circle, perhaps to die.

Instead of a goat, it was more likely that a human prisoner or convict might be the "guest of honor." Or maybe the French Army's lottery loser. Or some of the 20,000 captives taken by the Aztecs annually and ritually slain in order to maintain the people's murder-respecting relationship with their bloodthirsty gods.

The pyramid form *demands a victim*.
This is what we're not factoring into our thinking.

People in the bottom zone complaining of "the system" unconsciously feel this.

Watts is hardly a slum, yet the people rioted. I visited its nice little single-family houses with lawns several times while I puzzled on this. But the inhabitants felt a sense of compression to such a degree they exploded.

Ordinary Wars An Outlet

War is one of the ways nations work off their need to vent pent-up hatreds and thus feel cleansed.

The "enemy" is those Poles over there in 1939, when a few of their farmers attacked a few of our farmers at dawn today, therefore our army of three million—with 10,000 tanks and pieces of artillery which we just happened to have standing by in a neighboring field—crossed on a 500-mile front and soon took Warsaw.

The "glory" of victory.

Yes, unfortunately, war can make people feel good. It excites them. The death-thrust from above is shoved off onto someone else. Bands play.

WWII Nazi submariners early in the conflict had their "happy time" (as they called it for a while), sinking unarmed, unprotected merchantmen.

The death-outlet or blood-outlet at the bottom of the pyramid system cleanses it.

War causes the population to rally around and exalt the battle leaders on either side. Most of the towering leaders in history—good and bad—are identified with wars.

After WWII's forty million-plus deaths, the world's collective consciousness still had its bloodbaths: the formal Korea and Vietnam, and the less formal Java, Cambodia (some four million and counting), Masai, Uganda, and Hutu-Tutu slaughters, plus others.

The Pyramid's "Designated Victim" — Or D.V.

An example of a "Designated Victim" or D.V. is an innocent black in Mississippi in the 1920s caught and hung just because the general hatreds of a few of the population had to have an outlet—righteous and cleansing (even with the Bible quoted out of context and wildly extrapolated).

When pointing to others or telling jokes about them meets with reinforcement from friends, fellow workers, government, or whatever, the targets can begin to appear ripe for action. Guilt can lessen, and attacks break the surface in outright blocking, excluding, open snarling, damaging—even in talk of eradicating (all righteous, of course). The pot bubbles—and occasionally boils over.

Historically, Jews Were Often D.V.s

When nations needed dumping targets, they "righteously" hounded, tormented, killed, rounded up and impounded (or just as mysteriously, banished from the former impound areas) millions upon millions of Jews.

In the end-time, the Bible says everyone around Israel gangs up and attacks with intent to finish it off, but "the Lord was there" (Ezek. 35:10) and the aggressors get creamed so that it takes "seven months" (Ezek. 39:12) to bury them (perhaps even with bulldozers).

Black Africa Has Historically Also Been In A D.V. Role

Black Africa has been a D.V. for specific and non-specific collective hatreds looking for a place and population upon which to settle.

With much of the Western World's negatives pouring

down unannounced and unidentified, the tribes there psychologically have to dump, therefore pick on the neighboring tribe. The word "genocide" has been used frequently with regard to African tribal wars, beginning with the once-numerous and proud Masai.

India And Its Untouchables

India had its own many social strata, with the "untouchables" or outcasts at the bottom. The caste system is still a fact despite having been ruled illegal.

The word "untouchable" implies a gap. It says those people are psychologically outside the community. Although they're within the population, they've been driven out of the camp, so to speak.

And they're assigned what we used to call in the US Army "shit detail" of a perpetual kind. (Again, under the new laws, untouchability is illegal, but India is vast, and a recent TV interview with an Indian author revealed that the psychology of it and even the practice are still in effect .)

The Pyramid's "BM"

In the pyramid, people are "shit upon"—and this complaint is heard at many levels!

More History Of Sacrifice System

Long ago, when the sacrificial system first became popular in human thought, grain (for example) was burned at fall harvest-festival rituals. This was to partly satiate the gods' appetites for death (which appetites would soon be shown in the upcoming winter when everything would die).

If, as hoped, the fall offerings took the edge off the gods' appetites, the deities might cut the tribes some slack with a mild winter, or perhaps bring spring earlier.

However, despite the sacrifices (which included animals and humans), nature as well as life in general remained destructive.

Those doggoned volcanoes, also diseases, and attacks from other tribes, continued unabated.

Logically, tribespeople brought the worst grain and animals to the rituals, because the asset was going to be destroyed. Therefore, a new rule appeared: Not the worst, with little value to the sacrificer, but only the best was to be offered.

This concept soon grew to sacrificing innocent and pure humans.

Since many girls were killed at birth anyhow, young virgins were callously considered no real loss when tossed into volcanoes, or off the rocks, or whatever.

The murdering priests were of course not considered murderers but righteous, religious, godly.

In The Pyramid,
Kings Can Also Be Scapegoated

The scapegoat can even be the king, although this is unusual (see *The Golden Bough*).

Naturally, this is not practiced where the king is in a strong political or military position! Or where he might be in a mood to say, "All who believe I should be sacrificed shall be bound in their coats and their hosen, and tossed into the...."

However, even some strong kings in the feudal eras when there were hundreds of kings, took upon themselves the duty to be victimized for their people and, power or not, couldn't be kept from it.

Was there an escape valve? Oh sure. Often many went through sufferings and various steps of ritual debasement and killing, being rolled through the streets in a wagon in person or in effigy to be hooted at—or even made a target for stones or rotten vegetables—only to come out at the end of the week or fortnight of the religious days to resume the throne for the cleansed tribe.

Some priests did similar things. As with the kings, the priests did this for the people's sins, not for the many specific sins of the priests. Such "sacrificing" of priests was very rare, though, because it violated the principle!

Sinners Aren't Punished
By The Sacrifice System—Others Are

In all of the carnal mind's blame system, please note that sinners (individuals or tribes as a whole) are not really punished.

Say that again?

That's right—the entire reasoning and enactment was and is basically a shifting of the penalty onto someone or something else.

-

A Reminder

Before again picking up the text about Egypt, I would like to repeat my statement that the references concern the Bible metaphor and the *ancient empire* with its persecutions of Hebrews—not the Egyptian people or nation of today.

Three More Things Before We Leave "Egypt"

First, when the "two witnesses" (see previous chapter) are killed, they lie "in the street of the great city, which spiritually is called Sodom and Egypt, where also our Lord was crucified" (Rev. 11:8). Nothing in the Bible has any lower ranking on earth than this reference to "Sodom and Egypt."

Second, Egypt is often biblically synonymous with mammon.

Finally, Egypt is biblically cast as an enemy of Israel— in any of the forms or meanings of the word Israel.

< >

7
MORE EMPIRE CONCEPTS: ASSYRIA, BABYLON, PERSIA

II

Assyria

War And Expansion; Oppression Of The Jews

Waves of conquest by Assyrian kings such as Shalmaneser III, Tiglath-pileser III, Sargon II, and Sennacherib, swept the Middle East over a total, erratic period of more than 250 years from the 880s B.C. The capital of the ancient empire was at Nineveh on the upper Tigris in today's northern Iraq, now only ruins.

At its greatest extent under Ashurbanipal (669-626 B.C.), Assyria covered the Fertile Crescent from the head of the Persian Gulf well up into today's Turkey, then down along the Canaan coast (with Judah, Josiah's Kingdom, cut out), and into Egypt. It fell at last in 612 B.C. to the Babylonians and Medes, who destroyed Nineveh permanently.

Today's maps showing the empire's extent don't mean solid occupation such as found in World War II, or continuous occupation for the entire period. There was a lot of surging back and forth over the two and a half centuries.

Was Jerusalem under the Assyrians? Yes and no. The city was in Judah, which was not occupied (although Israel, the northern of the two Hebrew kingdoms, adjacent, had been conquered). Despite being allowed to retain its priestly government and some other freedoms, Judah nonetheless essentially belonged to Assyria, one source explains.

Sargon II carried off nearly 30,000 Jewish captives circa 722 B.C., an act which is said to have effectively ended the northern kingdom.

Assyria's special spirit would seem to be protracted and intractable warlikeness and expansion, coupled with oppression of the Jews.

III

Babylon

Mental Evil And Evil Science;
Oppression Of Israel; Warlike Expansion

Babylon is in today's Iraq on the Euphrates River. A few miles north and a short distance east, along the Tigris River, is today's Baghdad.

Babylon rebelled against Assyria with the aid of the Medes to the north, eliminated Nineveh forever, then set up its own empire.

Like Assyria at its peak, the Babylonian Empire covered an expanded Fertile Crescent, up into Turkey a bit, down Canaan's coast, into Egypt. Unlike Assyria, it occupied Jerusalem and (in the wickedest blow) destroyed Solomon's Temple in 586 B.C., after Zedekiah's revolt.

It was a hater of Israel then (and is a hater now).

Babylon was strong in the sciences, math, astronomy. Also evil sciences or sciences of evil such as the occult, war sciences used to hurt and oppress, and twisted reasoning. (See end-time references below from Revelation.) Astrology (spoken against in the Bible) was highly developed.

Of course, Babylon was pagan (as were Assyria and Egypt).

It's interesting to realize that in ancient times the Hebrews alone of all peoples officially worshiped one God (although unofficially, once away from the priests, many followed multiple gods. An example of Hebrew straying occurred on the Exodus when, in Moses' absence, the people made and worshiped a golden calf).

In a blow second only to their destruction of the Temple, the Babylonians carried off three groups of Judeans —10,000 at the beginning, many thousands more after a revolt, and finally, after more trouble, a third group. This *removed the bulk of the remaining Jews* from the area.

The Babylonian Empire didn't last long by ancient standards, only seventy-odd years, from 612 to 539 B.C.

In Revelation's end-time prophecies, Babylon is the term for the embodiment of evil involved in the second and final great defeat of evil.

(As I see it, evil's *first* great defeat is the primarily physical "Armageddon," which may actually be a "rolling" event in whose foothills we've been for decades; but which I agree will almost certainly come to a major climax.)

The second (or possibly concurrent) great defeat of evil seems to be more of a mental thing, involving "MYSTERY, BABYLON THE GREAT, THE MOTHER OF HARLOTS AND ABOMINATIONS OF THE EARTH" (Rev. 17:5). I think this is the biblical carnal mind itself ("enmity against God"—Rom. 8:7).

"Babylon The Great" (which is not the woman of chapter 12) sits on the beast with seven heads identified as seven kings. (These are probably the seven Bible empires, or seven challenges to God.)

This woman is "drunken with the blood of the saints, and with the blood of the martyrs of Jesus."

She "sitteth upon many waters" as well as on the heads of (more) kings—and the waters are described as "peoples, and multitudes, and nations, and tongues."

Further, she is identified as "that great city"(obviously the *opposite* of "the holy city, new Jerusalem" of Rev. 21). This Babylonian evil city "reigneth over the kings of the earth" before falling (Rev. 18).

So what are we to make of all this?

I believe Babylon symbolizes the biblical carnal mind "sitting on" everything as a framework other than the divine city, to wit: the world in its own mental image.

Its fall is the defeat of the mental essence of evil.

Babylon's most profound spirit is mental evil, if Revelation's prophecies are anywhere near true.

Add to that Babylon's scientific bent, and the ancient land represents evil science or scientific evil.

Some have openly said the US is the latter-days Babylon. I don't think so.

Although the US has certainly allowed hedonism to make great gains, I'll stick with my conviction that the heart of the US is spiritual and its existence ordained—also that it will come into a testing time where it will have to clean up its act if it is to go forward.

And go forward spiritually it will.

Contrariwise, the Babylonian concept is "the heart of darkness": evil and death instead of light and love as the ultimate powers at the center of deity. This is the carnal mind, not God—death, not life, as Paul said (Rom. 8:6).

IV

Persia

Belief In Material Resources

Persia, which had been expanding for a long time, took Babylon in 539 B.C.

A year later, Persia *allowed the Jews to return home.*

This Persian "nice guy" policy, employed throughout the huge new empire, often allowed conquered peoples to do their cultural things as far as practical—a program opposite to that of the Assyrians and Babylonians.

But Persia wasn't sweetness and light, and subjects who believed the conqueror wasn't in complete control could make fatal mistakes.

This biggest empire (to that time) stretched east beyond the Indus River (a traditional Indian border), north to the Aral Sea (east of the Caspian), then back west along the Caucasian mountains to cover all of present Turkey. It occupied Byzantium (later to become Constantinople) and lands north of it, finally extending as far west as Macedonia. In Egypt, it pushed south along the Nile to below Thebes. West, it entered Libya as far as Benghazi, beyond World War II's famed Tobruk.

These vast holdings included Canaan.

Cyrus II (the "Great") called himself "King of the four corners of the Earth." There again we see the idea that this relatively small chunk of the globe (though colossal for its time) was the "world."

And now to the topic of material resources.

The Bible tells us of the poverty-stricken widow about to surrender her collateralized sons to a lender. Elisha instructed her to gather many pots for olive oil, then start pouring from her tiny remaining stock. She poured and poured, filling all the containers. With this she paid her debt, and lived from the rest.

Scripture shows us repeatedly that there's a divine reality which is the real substance.

Moses' people on the Exodus were supplied by manna. Water came from a rock.

Jesus fed multitudes, and had more left over at the end than at the beginning. He knew the higher realm, and the effect it had on the material realm.

(The change in the human condition as the result of encountering the higher reality is the theme of this book.)

The Power Of Today's Pipeline

The industrial world's power and control may be awesome but it's utterly dependent on a dangerously long and fragile "pipeline," so to speak.

Europe imports some eighty percent of its oil from the Middle East, the US some sixty percent from all sources.

A shutoff by the Middle East could rearrange the entire structure of the world's economy. Nations could dry up in the manner that towns did when bypassed by the railroads.

The present Gulf states—Iraq, Iran, Saudi Arabia, Kuwait, and the Emirates—possess most of the easily-accessible petroleum in the world. It's there in huge pools convenient to pump.

If the Mideast goes to war, the time may come when we'll believe we need more petroleum, just as the widow believed she needed more olive oil.

But in divine reality, we'll need only more understanding of what Jesus said we didn't see or hear.

Oil In Bible Prophecy?

Petroleum doesn't *directly* appear in the ancient-empire Bible descriptions because it wasn't in demand then. However, it *indirectly* appears in *general* Mideast prophecy.

Ezekiel tells us of "the Assyrian." We know that Assyria was in today's Iraq, but was Ezekiel talking about a person from that land or a much wider region? Since "Pharaoh" is also mentioned, the prophecies could mean a group of Arab nations.

"The waters made him [the Assyrian] great...set him on high with her rivers...and sent out her little rivers unto all the trees of the field.... ...under his shadow dwelt all great nations...for his root was by great waters.... Take up a lamentation for Pharaoh...thou...troublest the waters...and fouledst their rivers.... By the swords of the mighty will I cause thy multitude to fall...neither shall the foot of man trouble them any more.... Then I will make their waters deep, and cause their rivers to run like oil, saith the Lord God" (Ezek. 31 and 32).

So the rivers and waters going out to all would appear to really be oil—and after threats to the "great nations" there is war.

After which the rivers again "run like oil. "

Certainly the US and EU have contingency plans based on potential trouble with the "rivers" that run out "unto all the trees of the field" and cause "all great nations" to dwell under the shadow of the Assyrian.

Prophecy Browsing

Ezekiel from about chapters 29 through 39 contains several prophecies regarding the end times in the Mideast. These passages make interesting reading.

Some of the visions cover a wider period of time and area of geography than others. The resulting overlap means that one vision may not take up where the other leaves off.

In one prophecy, a group comes against Israel and is defeated in such a way that "Egypt" cannot be occupied for some "forty years" thereafter—which some say suggests radiation from nuclear weapons.

In another, the Russians come in for the purpose of keeping the peace but instead "take a spoil. " This plunder is probably oil. Since Russia is presently broke, it could easily be covetous of the wealth and power of the oil nations.

Terrible battles are predicted. After one, it takes "seven months" to bury the bodies and "seven years" to burn the spears for firewood. (I don't know where spears would fit into modern warfare but apparently some weapon will burn and give heat—maybe a small incendiary rocket.)

The EU In The Thick Of It?

Europe's present dependency on Persian Gulf oil could explain why interpreters of Bible prophecy believe the EU will figure large in the big showdown there.

If the EU becomes the risen "Rome" (see a later chapter), it's supposed to attack Israel. By aiding the Arab attack, it could both help its oil situation and renew its historic oppression of the Jews.

England, with some independent oil reserves mainly in the North Sea, and an enormous amount of coal, isn't as utterly dependent on the Persian Gulf as is the EU proper.

Japan needs Persian Gulf oil to survive. Knowing its weakness in this area, it constantly seeks more East Indies oil while developing reserves in Australia.

Regarding the US, I've always said it would commandeer Caribbean and Mexican oil if necessary, and get by.

God-protected as always, the US will find itself suffering, sweating, praying—and climbing.

Is the biblically-predicted world-threatening conflict over what appears to be oil, the same as the biblically-predicted world-threatening conflict over Israel?

I doubt these are identical, but they're in the overall end-time package together.

< >

8
EMPIRE V WAS GREECE

V

Greece

Greece Gave Us Western Civilization
Or Culture

On The Plus Side:
   Early Forms Of Democracy;
   The Greek Alphabet; Love Of Art,
   Architecture, Letters, Law, Discussion

On The Minus Side:
   Its Mythological Hero Man—
      Which Odysseus Started, But Ain't
      The Man Christ Jesus Is Trying
      To Show The World;
   Pagan-Myth Gods And Goddesses;
   And Wars

Did Western Civilization Begin
With Mycenaean Greece And Troy
1450-1150 B.C.?

As discussed earlier, Western Culture didn't begin in Mycenaean Greece, despite the legends of Troy. That era contributed, but wasn't the beginning.

Mycenae (today's Mykinai, located some sixty miles west of Athens), was the successor to Crete, the granddaddy of Aegean powers. The campaigns to defeat Troy made the times memorable, although the most famous item, the Greek Horse, might have been fictional.

Troy, not large, is remembered mainly due to Homer's *Iliad* (although that ends before the horse and the fall), and his *Odyssey* (where the horse appears), and the much-later *Aeneid* by Virgil of Rome (also telling of the horse).

One source identifies nine Troys from 3000 B.C. to A.D. 400. Eratosthenes selected 1194 B.C. for the most famed fall and the horse.

The Mycenaean period, which ended with the Dorian invasions about 1150 B.C., was a forerunner of Western Culture, but not a start.

Did Western Civilization Begin With
Homer (800s B.C.), Or Other Early
Writers And Literature, Or Artists And Arts?

Cultural streams moving towards the later centuries made significant contributions but weren't the origin.

However, what about Homer in particular? Some have suggested he could be our beginning as well as a central emblem of early literature and the arts.

Unfortunately, Homer appears to have been several poets writing over a period of time from 1159 to 685 B.C., born in seven different places.

Homeric poetry rather than Homer was the thing, *Encyclopedia Britannica* tells us, adding, "The poems are facts and 'Homer' a hypothesis to account for them." Hmm.

The poems certainly included plenty of fiction. After all, they had to be read to audiences in theaters, and one had to hold one's audience.

So when were Homer's *Iliad* and *Odyssey* written? In the 800s B.C., probably. (Please note that this is at least 300 years after a popular date for the fall of Troy, so the stories weren't eyewitness accounts.)

(The *Aeneid*, which also told us about Troy, was written by a Roman, Publius Vergilius Maro—Virgil to you, also spelled Vergil—some *1100 years* after the possible events, drawing heavily from Homer's *Iliad*. See the next chapter for more about Aeneas, Virgil's main character, a wanderer the author would have us believe left Troy, landed on Italy's west coast, and became the pre-founder of Rome.)

Suffice it to say that Homer's works won't support a "starting date" for Western Culture; however, all early letters and arts were definitely important cultural tributaries moving into later centuries.

Did Western Civilization Begin With The Olympics In The 700s B.C.?

Although interesting and definitely part of the "pre-beginning" of Western Civilization, the Olympics, which were first held in Olympia in the 700s B.C., aren't the point of ignition for a culture as vast, diverse, dynamic and long-lasting as the Western.

Did Western Civilization Begin When
Alexander Hellenized The World
He'd Conquered In The 300s B.C.?

Alexander "Hellenized" or at least attempted to "make Greek" many subjugated cultures. The program began during his short life and extended through the empires he divided to his generals. Although memorable, and leaving evidence identifiable even today, this wasn't our launch pad.

Did Western Civilization Begin With
The Athens Of Pericles In The 400s B.C.?

Yes. Here we can make a case.

Western Culture finds its foundation in the midst of a peacetime Athens of government, law, architecture, art, literature, philosophy and lively discussion.

"Power rests with the majority instead of a few." Those vital words by Pericles his 431 B.C. oration bring Greece forward through more than two millennia to the US.

Athens' best five decades began in about 479 B.C. when the Persian threat receded, and lasted until after the Peloponnesian War started in 431. The "Golden Age of Pericles" occupied some thirty years 459-429 B.C. when he was the city-state's most influential citizen. He died in 429.

Coming to flower in Pericles' Athens were many elements which had significant earlier beginnings, including art, architecture, written language and the alphabet, literature (including tragedy, comedy, philosophy, history, and poetry), and new concepts in government by the people.

Let's take a brief look at these great cultural elements, holding government until last in order to discuss it at more length.

Arts And Architecture: The incredible architecture of the Greeks, which started centuries before Pericles, reached its peak during his time when he rebuilt the Acropolis after war damage, and constructed the Parthenon.

To this day we copy Greek architecture, significantly for our main government and university buildings. We admire the designers, builders, and artisans (who could carve those columns and "capitals" such as the leafy Corinthian).

Graceful Greek statues predate Michaelangelo, Da Vinci, and Bernini by sometimes more than 2,000 years.

The Alphabet: The famous Greek alphabet is a daily part of our Western Culture today. Too, some *twelve percent of English words* are directly derived from the Greek, says TIME-LIFE.

(Earlier, we took a look at the evolvement of the alphabet, the transitional tool which was as vital to the spread of language as the much later movable type. The alphabet brought vast expansion and mobility to language by enabling the phonetic construction of words and then sentences from only a handful of sound-symbols instead of from the clumsy, hopelessly slow, nuance-less, too-numerous, difficult to write and teach, picture-grams in their various forms.)

The Greek alphabet came from Phoenician Script in the 8th century B.C., from *aleph* and *beth* into *alpha* and *beta*. The Greeks improved what they got. Greek went into Latin, and Latin into the European languages including English.

Literature: All forms started long before the Golden Age, but emerged strongly during and after.

Prodigious writers, the Greeks are still studied in the present.

Of 150 tragedians, only a few works by three survive: seven plays of eighty-two by Aeschylus (d. 456 B.C.); seven of 123 by Sophocles (d. 406 B.C.); nineteen of ninety-two by Euripides (d. 406 B.C.).

Of 170 comedy writers, only a few works by Aristophanes (d. ca 388 B.C.), and Menander (d. 292 B.C.) have made it to the present.

Of philosophical works, all by Plato (d. 348 or 347 B.C.) are available. (Plato and Xenophon set down the philosophy of Socrates [d. 399], who didn't write.)

All the histories by Herodotus (d. between 430 and 420 B.C.) and Thucydides (d. ca 401 B.C.) survive.

We touched on Greek poetry earlier.

The real "Greek tragedy" was war. Greeks couldn't keep from attacking others, or, of necessity, defending themselves from invaders. There was bloodletting after bloodletting, century after century.

We can only guess how much art, architecture and literature was destroyed in wars, and how much was never produced due to energies diverted to wars, or because promising creative people were killed.

The Golden Age was a peaceful period between the Persian and Peloponnesian wars—a fact contributing greatly to its success.

New Concepts In Government By The People: Rudimentary democratic concepts and practices barely preceded Pericles; however, those and other forerunners were important. For example, open exchange of opinions was acceptable, judges tempered the laws, and courts heard legal arguments (things not permitted under absolute rulers).

Greeks long prior to the Golden Age could define types of government, such as monarchy, also oligarchy (rule by a few). There was the "lord" (original word for which was "tyrant"). (At first, a tyrant was not necessarily evil, but later apparently earned the reputation for "tyranny.")

Laws existed (and could be changed) long before the Golden Age. For a time, an appointed "lawmaker" made the laws, keeping in mind certain criteria including tradition, past decisions and so on. Draco's laws were too tough (hence our word "draconian"), leading the later Solon to repeal many (resulting in our word "solon" applied to judges today in approval of the original Solon's wisdom).

Town-meeting types of public assemblies were forerunners of more citizen participation.

Athenian Democracy

The *developing idea of democracy* came to its first realization in Athens, but it wasn't what we believe it to have been (see below), and it didn't last.

Whereas some in Greece had dreamed of a pure democracy, the net result was only a sort of republic. Nonetheless, the concepts were powerful and the attempts important.

Only some *ideals* came forward through two millennia of Western-world governmental turmoil to 1776 America. I believe the US founding and practice drew far more heavily on inspiration from God than from the Greeks; but undeniably, the *idea of majority rule* was first espoused and attempted as a government on this planet by the Greeks.

The West, later throwing off its monarchies, dictators both fascist and communist, military juntas, and so on, has essentially produced one good "democracy-based republic" (the US), some limited ones, and some poor ones.

How Good Was Athenian Democracy?

Pericles himself is reputed to have said that Athenian democracy existed in theory, while the practice was rule by the first citizen.

So let's take a look at the forms of Athenian democracy, and how they functioned.

The Assembly

Cleisthenes in 507 B.C. (about thirty years before the end of the Persian wars and fifty years before Pericles) revised the constitution to provide that all adult male citizens were auto-matically members of the Assembly.

There was freedom of speech and equality before the laws; however, females (as in the later original US system) weren't in government and in fact had few rights, although they could inherit.

About three years before Pericles, Ephialtes in 462 B.C. stripped the aristocrats of special powers. In response they killed him, but the reforms survived.

The Assembly was now the basic political body.

The Council (500 Men) Became Necessary

The Assembly met forty times a year in an amphitheater. Having no electronic amplification, the special acoustics of the amphitheater aided budding democracy.

Since "all adult male citizens" couldn't possibly have fitted onto the seats, it was a good thing that only interested parties attended these Assembly meetings.

Because anyone was allowed to speak on any subject, it was necessary to have an agenda prepared by a *council of 500* men, fifty from each of the ten Attic tribes. They were elected—in a manner of speaking—by *lot,* and their terms were limited.

However, it was soon discovered that even a council of 500 men was too unwieldy. This led to the smaller, more manageable fifty-man inner council (see the next section below), although of course the larger council was retained.

The Inner Council Of Only Fifty Men

Fifty men comprised the inner council or "prytany," which met each day. They ran the government.

The makeup changed *ten times each year.*

Chosen by the larger council, it was headed, however, by one person taken from a rotating group of ten *generals* picked by the Assembly for one-year terms and reelectable.

The person filling this chairmanship was essentially the CEO of Athens.

However, he was changed...*every day.*

Would you repeat that please? I seem to have missed something.

Yes, I'll drive it by again. The top person was changed *every day.*

Athenians feared any one person getting too much power.

All This Was A Democracy?

Not really, but it was a start.

It was the world's laboratory for earliest democracy.

Where Did Pericles Fit Into All This?

He was both a member of the Assembly and a general apparently perennially reappointed to the group of ten generals to head the prytany. Thus he sat in the official seat at least every tenth day, but in effect more.

His ideas and oratory made him the leader of Athens.

His great-uncle was the constitutionalist Cleisthenes, who had produced the broad-based Assembly. Therefore Pericles was an insider not someone unknown.

Cleisthenes had left the privileged with special powers. Ephialtes got rid of the powers, further paving the way for democracy, but paying with his life for his valuable reforms.

When the pure democracy proved unmanageable, the strange republic came into place. Pericles made things work.

From his life came his interesting remark that Athenian democracy was in fact rule by the "first citizen."

The age became identified with Pericles' name.

Slave Population

Citizens had time for civic affairs because slaves took care of things for them while they argued. Athens' population in 430 B.C. was over 300,000, including 100,000 slaves.

The Importance Of The Individual

Despite flaws in the practical Athenian democracy when contrasted with its ideals, I won't take away from the Greeks' vital early concepts of the importance of the individual and the dignity of the self-rule concept—things which deeply impressed the best elements of Western thought and were part of the beginning of Western Civilization.

As for the US level of democracy in actual practice, Greece stimulated our thought, but is hardly a foundation.

The Greeks drew on their "gods" and human aspirations for their democracy, while US democracy is an expression of our spiritual sense of one God as variously seen by our population.

John Adams is reputed to have said a democracy can exist only where there is a moral foundation—and by that he probably meant the Judeo-Christian Commandments (hopefully in a solonic interpretation, not the draconian versions given me as a youngster). The Greeks were pagans, and their temples were to pagan deities—utterly mythological.

-

And Now For A Brief Discussion
Of The Minuses Involved In Greece's
Role Of Founding Western Civilization

The minuses include the entire cult of the invincible personal-power man (or woman—but mainly man).

Found throughout ancient times, this was certainly embraced in Greece and has become a rampant part of Western Culture, leading the onslaught of secularization.

Essentially, it's "ye shall be as gods" instead of the image of God—the serpent's prophecy in Genesis fulfilled.

The indestructible hero who doesn't call on God (and who fills our entertainment) is part of the predicted end-time falling-away from God.

The human hero rescuing a child from a burning building is in a different category: real life actions by frail, and often praying, mortals.

People such as David in the Bible were heroic, but they relied on God.

Another Greek minus was the panoply of gods and goddesses in addition to their personal-power man.

· In line with this, Western Culture today has more gods, goddesses, and idols in the image of man than ever before in history, as secular, even hedonistic, trends accelerate.

Some are living idols from entertainment including sports, while others are from business and finance. Or in the case of some sports figures, all four categories.

Some are utterly mythological film and TV "heroes" and cartoon and toy "super-heroes" human and animal, in a proliferation that's just astonishing.

Can such things fit into a West which is Judeo-Christian (and some Islamic)...*monotheistic?* One wouldn't think so, but thus far they're not just fitting in but multiplying and taking over.

Today or tomorrow, can any of these things "arise and save" you?

Goddess Of Fortune— Not Personified, But...Everywhere

In the US and worldwide we see the incredible increase in worship of the "goddess of fortune" or "lady luck."

Even in my "non-gambling" state, every convenience store is a casino with machines issuing glamorous lottery tickets. Local TV newscasts feature the selections, announce the results, and run strips at the bottom of reports.

Las Vegas, the world's symbol of gambling, has something from each ancient empire, in advanced forms.

It has Egypt's pyramid (and Sphinx). Another example of the pyramidal form is gambling itself, with a few winners at the top, a vast bottom of losers, a lot of strugglers in between. Vegas also has Egypt's mammon in the form of money-worship. Babylon is represented by cynical, if not evil, sciences controlling every game in the house's favor and literally selling "gain" for a few based on the misfortunes of many who had sought the same false goal. Rome provides Caesar and hedonism. From all the ancients there are star-gods and idols in saturation quantities. Again from all there's expansion—gambling fever taking over vast portions of the globe plus electronic media and entertainment. Also from the past, Vegas has intense hypnotic influences such as whirling machines, amazing designs and lights, and captivating entertainment engaging the senses so they don't seek God and therefore don't get the "Israel" change.

Some gamblers pray to win. The gods churn and redistribute the pools of gambling money (some cruelly lost, some happily abandoned), but does *God* do this—God who has divine abundance for everybody?

And Now To The Final Greek Minus: War

From the beginning, the little Aegean Sea was a cauldron of fighting.

I'd like to report that Greece wasn't bloodily expansionist (as the others were) but Alexander captured as much territory as Persia, and more than the others.

Is Greek warlikeness part of Western Culture? Certainly—along with everyone's personal warlikeness.

Defense is necessary, of course. But there were so many wars that it was often an action-reaction scene difficult to sort out, like Athens and Sparta.

Did Greece Make War On The Jews?

Alexander's empire included Judea. Later, his successors also held the Jews' homeland.

However, Greek oppression had a deeper aspect. Its "Hellenization" program almost put the Jews out of business by trying both forcefully and subtly to change their unique identity.

Successfully rebelling against this Hellenization were the Maccabees, establishing the Hasmonean Jewish Kingdom 165-63 B.C. (102 years) and even getting the Roman Senate to agree.

Did the twin approach of the Greeks—both subtle and harsh—work its way into Western Culture? Yes. The West has used plenty of subtle erasure and assimilation against Jewish identity while also using as much outright ferocity, or more, as any of the ancient empires.

Jews openly speak of their special effort to maintain their racial and religious identity.

< >

9
EMPIRE VI WAS ROME

VI

Rome

World Conquest; Oppression Of The Jews

It's been said that Rome is the heritage of the US and the West; however despite her many important contributions, I believe she is disqualified as a basis or co-basis because she lived the very reverse of the key essence: "Power rests with the majority instead of a few."

Beneath her shining exterior, a consistently aggressive spirit conquered, oppressed, or enslaved everything in sight. Unhappily, this nature identified ancient Rome.

Many contend that the early republic makes Rome at least a full partner with Greece in basing Western Culture. Some laudable ideals were there, but the practice was "business as usual," as explained later in this chapter.

No matter how many positive things from Rome we use in our lives today—and Rome had many pluses to go with her minuses—it's not possible for something as uncivil as the 1,000 years of western Rome's existence (B.C. and A.D.) to be the basis for our civilization.

One major source, even while trying to sing Rome's praises, admitted that we idealize her less the more we know about her.

Let's Look At Rome's Many Pluses

Engineering And Architecture: Some of Rome's positives can be seen in aqueducts and bridges. One stone bridge 600 feet long and 200 high is still in use in Spain. Aqueducts are visible although no longer usable with the exception of one small stretch maintained for historical purposes.

The Coliseum also exemplifies Rome's mastery of the arch.

(Roman arches were so advanced that the concept did not enter a new phase until long after her fall, when Gothic cathedrals circa 1200 used arched roofs atop high, thin walls kept from pushing outward by "flying buttresses.")

Fifty thousand miles of stone-block military highways, plus 200,000 miles of secondary roads connected the Roman empire. Again, parts of these can still be viewed. Of course, most of the construction was in other people's lands, enabling troops to move quickly to maintain their suppression. Commerce, though, was also facilitated.

Romans get credit for discovering and using concrete. Mortar gets stronger the longer it sets, hence many monuments still standing. Cement enabled the construction of great pillars for bridges, water aqueducts and the like, and strong, high walls able to support major roofs.

We benefit from Roman architecture's *dome* to cover wide spans. (Egypt's "hypostyle" halls had rows of columns supporting flat roofs, their beams of stone or wood being short. Greece, when limited by the length of stone beams, obtained long timbers to construct gable roofs for temples. But nothing compared with the span of the dome.)

Rome's 142-foot diameter Pantheon is *still intact* after nearly 1900 years—the model for later domes worldwide.

Art And Sculpture: Rome was impressive in continuing and adding to western art and sculpture. (We should note here that the famed art, sculpture, and buildings of the Renaissance weren't Roman, coming some 1,000 years later.)

Rule By Law: This *ideal* emerged from Rome's Republic and even its Empire period. However, it wasn't the practice except where it suited the rulers or pacified the masses. Lip service, though, was prevalent.

A second important ideal was that the top figures themselves were controlled by the framework of laws. This again was great for lip service and oratory by rulers, political leaders, generals, and parties, but in practice it was usually gotten around.

One interesting element of Roman law was that perhaps for the first time anywhere, some of the laws were written by the people. By comparison, Sumerians and Babylonians had law codes dictated by rulers. Hebrews had law codes given, the priests naturally said, directly by God (although Jesus overturned part of that when he rebuked "eye for an eye," even while he ratified part of it when he upheld the Commandments.) Greece's laws came from appointed "lawgivers" who were respectful of common or "unwritten" law, existing statutes, and the times (which might even have involved political pressure by the people).

Roman laws were not nearly as accessible by the masses as we believe they were.

The practice of Roman law wasn't one-tenth as glorious as we think, although the ideals were great.

(See further comment on Roman law below under the "republic".)

Our Language: A major Roman plus is our language. As traced earlier in this book, our roots came west from the Middle East to Greece, then to Italy to become Latin, which in time formed the basis for the European Romance languages, which influenced English and finally "American."

Literature: All forms of literature were highly respected, expanded and perpetuated by Rome.

Durable Figures: Many Roman figures from all fields are still studied in the present.

Permanent Marks Over A Wide Area: Rome profoundly influenced surroundings and customs, leaving permanent evidence of her presence as far north as Britain, in most of western Europe, and along North Africa's rim.

-

Now Let's Look At Rome's Many Minuses

Conqueror, Enslaver: Rome conquered most of the world known to the West, and lived off slaves and tribute from those lands.

Having studied Rome's life, behavior, militarism, government, leaders, decadence, and decline since schooldays (and topped it all off with *I Claudius*), it's a puzzle to me why we glorify Rome; and a bigger puzzle why we believe it to be the heritage of our great, free nation, although other parts of the West may see it differently.

Hitler called Rome the First Reich, Napoleon (another disaster to Europe although still glorified instead of condemned) the Second, and named his own brief and terrible empire the "Third Reich." He hoped it (like Rome) would last 1,000 years. Hitler's emulation of Rome is hardly a recommendation for it.

Although it was only a movie, Demetrius the slave in *The Robe* raged about Rome's dark side to Marcellus the tribune, "Masters of the world, you call yourselves! Thieves! Murderers! Jungle animals!" Lines, yes, but all too true.

We can't discount that many in our society today admire Rome's military organization and efficiency, about which more below.

Many also admire the social structure of an educated and wealthy elite essentially running things. For those admirers, all of that gives off a certain light.

As the result of Vietnam and Watergate, the mood of the US has shifted from not scrutinizing its government to almost overdoing it. We now seem willing to also reexamine the past and our positions regarding the past.

Persecution Of Jews: Rome invaded the Jewish homeland and controlled it for centuries. It persecuted the population, participated in the execution of Jesus, crushed rebellions, destroyed the Second Temple, scattered the peoples.

Persecution Of Christians: At first, Jesus and his followers were called Jews (and Jesus wasn't identified as a

Christian but accused of being king of the Jews). Later, the word "Christian" came into use (Acts 11:26). Before and after, the disciples and other followers were persecuted and often killed.

Rome finally accepted Christianity; however, the approved form had been purged of the healing and changing aspect which so threatened the world's (Rome's) system.

The Gladiatorial Concept: Mortal combat, where only one is left standing, performed in great arenas, brought the Egyptian pyramid's organizational form to a new level of activity and violence. We see more than hints of this in today's business, sports, litigiousness, ferocity instead of cooperation, family squabbles, and condo associations.

Mythological Gods And Goddesses: Pagan gods and goddesses abounded. Rome had a panoply of imaginary deities to which it erected temples and for which the population held festivals and rituals.

Humans were elevated to "gods." A few leaders bestowed this status upon themselves, a few accepted it when conferred by government, while a few others just imagined themselves to be "gods."

Rome's Military Might—Both Admirable And Not: The entire Roman Empire wasn't self-supporting or creative in the sense of being an entity in and of itself, but existed by knocking the other fellow in the head and taking what he had.

From beginning to end, Roman armies roamed far beyond their home base for the purpose of oppression and theft. Soldiers also built the great road system of Europe of that time, but 50,000 miles of it were military roads to quickly move troops and maintain control.

All this was the darkest side of a brilliant military.

Yet we admire Rome's legions.

We admire efficiency, color, authority—we can't help it. Movies and artwork have glamorized the crimson cloth, the body-shaped armor.

We admire the fighting abilities of Roman soldiers, the teamwork of the legions' special battle formations (successors to the Greek/Macedonian phalanx) and their "tortoise" (which can be seen in action in the movie *Cleopatra*).

Perhaps if Julius Caesar had never lived, we'd perceive Rome's legions darkly, but even Caesar's enemies admired him!

He ranks today as one of the world's greatest generals. (He's sometimes confused with his heir and grandnephew Octavian, also known as Augustus Caesar, son of Caesar, or just "Augustus," who ruled for forty-one years after him.)

Julius' embodiment of the spirit of battle, which so aroused his men, and his frequent presence in the middle of the fighting (which drew a cheer even from the enemy in one engagement) put today's still-indelible mark of glory on Roman arms.

His organizational and motivational skills, training capabilities, control of maneuver in combat, and quality of fighting men were not found again until the pre-Stalingrad Wehrmacht.

Yes, even in this century we've admired our enemies: The Red Baron, Rommel, the Me109 airplane, the astonishing fighting ability of the German soldier.

Tough General DeGaulle at the Stalingrad memorial said, "An amazing people." The Russians thought he meant them, but he said, "The Germans—to have come this far."

Caesar's use of engineering in battles, which were often sieges, was unmatched in history to his time.

He employed siege towers, and siege "engines" that hurled rocks, poles, and javelins toward enemies either behind walls or massed in the field.

For one of Caesar's battles, the men erected two concentric rings of logs like fences, one thirteen miles around and the other nine and a half miles. The inner ring enabled the siege of the city, while the outer provided defense against attacks from neighboring areas. The ability to motivate soldiers to build such astonishing fortifications has not been found elsewhere.

Nonetheless, Caesar fought wars of aggression, slaughtering people defending their own lands.

Under any of their generals, Roman common soldiers often engaged in construction.

Note the huge size of the blocks that made up the high, arched aqueducts, and the substantial cubes more than a foot on edge, set solid for Roman roads. Many were cut and installed by the legions.

Since it was a common practice to let troops have enemy prisoners as slaves, I imagine there was some help.

But is aggression, conquest, and enslavement right under any circumstances?

In our discussion of Roman pluses and minuses, where does the *republic* fit? We'll take this up in the section immediately following.

-

The Roman Republic—
A Plus, A Minus, Or A Draw?

A draw. From hard facts (not from the many legends or ideals which overstate the republic), I couldn't call it either a plus or a minus—just an "even. "

Many consider the republic to have been a major contributor to the democracy-based US republic and to individual rights then and now. But did it earn that place, or have we glamorized it and bestowed our own wishes upon it?

Although most of the reasons for the nostalgia escape me, I emphatically credit three things: the ideals; the important series of attempts (despite the fact that all produced unstable results); and the overall experiment with its many phases (changing often) over five centuries (all B.C.).

Certainly the US picked up some pluses from all this, but the ancient republic's proof of its own concepts was seriously lacking. (The US obtained much more from God than from Rome, proved by both our stability and progress.)

The Roman Republic wasn't a single entity but changeable—and none of its forms held together. Rulers, not the people, ran things, and before the end, dictators. There were popular uprisings. Nonetheless, the concept gripped minds. When emperors finally took over, they spouted oratory of the *republic,* to appeal to the people and also hide the fact that (by that time) the republic was "history" (and was never what its enunciators and later historians claimed for it).

Also notice the order of events: Instead of the people rising and setting up self-rule, emperors took over from the shattered, incompetent republic, and installed an empire.

A Quick Overview Of Republic And Empire

Rome's republic and later empire each covered about 500 years. Thus nearly 1,000 years elapsed from the beginning of self-rule in 509 B.C. until the collapse of the Western Empire in A.D. 476.

But the *founding* of the town on the Tiber came nearly 250 years before self-rule, in 753 B.C. Who controlled from then until 509? We have no answer before 600, but know that Etruscan kings then held sway until overthrown in 509.

From 509 until 27 B.C., when Octavian became the first emperor of Rome (about 482 years), the republic was in effect; however, in its last 100 or more years, it existed in name only.

The empire then continued until A.D. 476 in the West (while the Eastern Empire, not part of this discussion, lasted yet another 1,000 years until Byzantium's fall in A.D. 1453.)

Does The Republic
Deserve Its Glorious Reputation?

No. "The Republic" is more of a handle for the *period* 509-27 B.C. than for the *government* or governments during those centuries of internal and external fighting, where leadership often changed hands by wars, coups, and assassinations, eradicating or driving out the opposition.

And all this time, we thought the place was smoothly governed by high-minded voting!

· The people didn't rule, that much was certain. Or elect those who did, except that after a while they could place tribunes and some others into the "gladiatorial contest" called "government."

Important Pluses From The Republic Were These:
Ideals; Attempts To Have People Make The Laws;
The Theory (Not Practice) Of Rule By Law;
At Least Rhetorical Respect For The Law;
Attempts At Assemblies To Represent The Mass;
The Bicameral System;
And Certain Citizens Such As Cincinnatus

The republic's *ideals* were excellent; however, in practice they weren't carried out, and attempts to carry them out were shaky at best. Nonetheless, I thoroughly applaud the ideals and attempts to make them practical.

Did the people make the laws? No, but again the ideal was there. During the tumultuous and varied experience called the republic, certainly some laws were made or heavily influenced by the people's representatives or parties—or by threats of rebellions or by actual outbreaks. Also, the people were able to deny some laws. The gravest flaw in the system was that too many leaders just overrode the laws.

Did the law or humans rule? It was "business as usual": politicians, generals and parties in power ruled. We've learned much from Roman law (and experiments) but powerful people and groups ruled, fought (literally) for control, and put their agendas first even while citing "the law" and "the people."

Was there respect for the law? Yes, as an ideal expounded in rhetoric. It dropped off sharply after that.

Several popular assemblies were elected or gathered from the mass or from its political parties. All proved unstable, as outlined in part later below. Nonetheless, the struggles and experiments are worthy of great admiration.

The "bicameral" legislative concept developed in the republic, although over a choppy course. Sometimes three major groups influenced legislation. No matter—anything was better than autocratic rule by one person or group. (The major Roman flaw of *a pair* of leaders at the top is discussed later. This attempt to avoid rule by *one* person undoubtedly caused more trouble than it prevented.)

In the bicameral systems of recent centuries, one body represents the mass, the other the class. This fundamental concept operated in Rome's republic in various forms.

When in history did the first elected popular assembly with teeth appear? Greece gets the credit, I believe; however, in a strange twist, their Assembly wasn't effective until the class took control.

We admire some of the people involved in Roman experiments with a republican form of government. Cincinnatus, a Roman soldier/statesman, was emulated by George Washington when he proffered his sword to the congress after the war before returning to his Virginia farm.

How much of the US founding came from Rome's republic? A recent article in *National Geographic* magazine cites instances from our struggle for independence in which some of our founders used at least some of the Roman ideals for part of their inspiration.

I would redirect attention to divine inspiration. The US democracy-based republic, although it drew some idealistic and practical bits and pieces from history, was inspired by higher things.

I would also point out the chasm between Rome's career of aggression, conquest, and enslavement (during all of the republic and empire periods), and the ultimate destiny of the US, which is the subject of this book.

-

How Did The Republic Get Started?
Let's Begin At The Founding Of Rome 753 B.C.

The first settlement was 244 years before self-rule began in 509.

Fact And Fiction About Rome's Founding

There are four concepts. Either of the first two could be true:
(1) Founded in 753 B.C. by Latins living in the area.
(2) Founded 753 B.C. by Etruscans.

The next two are purely fictional or mixtures of fiction and fact but so popularly circulated as to be taught in schools (with the caveat "legendary") and believed by many to be factual:
(3) In what sounds like a "stretch" to me, Virgil (writing in the first century B.C.) tries to connect Rome with Troy (1194 B.C.). In his *Aeneid*, Aeneas, son of "Venus," who had been defeated at Troy, does a sort of second *Odyssey* (Virgil was heavily influenced by the *Iliad*), and winds up...on the Italian west coast near the place where Rome would later (441 years later!) be founded.
In this story, the mother of Romulus and Remus is said to have descended from Aeneas.

And now the one you've all been waiting for:
(4) Romulus and Remus.
If Romulus was an actual figure inside all the legendary cloaking, then he was a *Latin*, and this founding concept would fit under (1) above, "founded in 753 B.C. by Latins."

The Latins' northern border was the south side of the Tiber. A Vestal Virgin of the Latins very unvirginally bore twin sons fathered by the god Mars (that's her story, anyhow).

The Latin king, her uncle, threw the infants onto the Tiber banks to die. Suckled by a wolf and later raised by a shepherd, at manhood they wanted to build a city on the Tiber.

To determine which of them should lay out the lines of this new city, they chose "divination." Romulus looking in one direction saw a dozen vultures, while Remus looking the other way saw only six. So Romulus marked the boundary with a plow (a traditional and sacred rite) in 753 B.C.

Then Remus, miffed, mocked it. In response, Romulus *killed* his brother, pronouncing, "So perish all who ever cross my walls."

Nice guy, this Romulus.

The Area Had A Long Prior History

The region around the once-puny town on the Tiber, as well as the rest of Italy, had a long but fuzzy history prior to the founding.

The population of the local area began with pre-historic tribespeoples (not the Latins) who continued to live in the general vicinity after the founding.

The Latins were one group from Indo-European tribes which had moved south into Northern Italy around 1000 B.C. and settled what became Latium, south of the Tiber.

These things are considered to be fact.

Around 800 B.C., Etruscans came from...where?... possibly Asia Minor, and settled well north of today's

Rome. They produced an interesting culture but detailed knowledge is limited due to a language still only partly deciphered. Expanding north to the Alps and head of the Adriatic, they also came south down the boot until stopped by the Greeks, who had settled in the foot and on Sicily.

Did they found Rome? No one yet knows for certain, but the probability is against them and in favor of the Latins.

Maybe when ancient Etruscan writing can finally be read, a document will tell of the founding of Rome.

The word Roma might not have come from Romulus at all, but was an Etruscan word (TIME-LIFE).

The Roman Republic Appears

From about 600 to 509 B.C., three Etruscan kings are said to have ruled Rome. Then the monarchy was overthrown and the early republic set up.

(We're still talking about a town, not even a hint of the Rome that would appear by stages.)

The people still believed in *rule from the top* (a king-like concept called *imperium*), with double consuls swinging most of the weight. Therefore from the start it wasn't a republic in today's sense.

It changed many times over its nearly 500-year existence, and we'll touch on some of the changes below.

Before proceeding, let's identify two heroes: Horatio and Cincinnatus (whose legends contain some solid fact, although difficult to separate from the fiction).

Horatio in about 500 defended the new republic's town against the advancing army of Lars Porsenna, who wanted to return the rule to Etruscan monarchs.

Standing at the far end of the bridge, he held off the enemy while the bridge was cut down behind him. In one variation of the legend he died; in another he dove into the water and maybe lived, maybe died; and in yet another he swam to safety. All agree a brave deed was done. Lars-baby didn't get into the town of Rome, and the fledgling republic or home-rule survived to live another day.

Cincinnatus lived about fifty years later, also in the early formative years of the republic. As mentioned earlier, he was a farmer given dictatorial powers to defeat an army of invaders. After dispatching them in but sixteen days, he relinquished his powers, new political potential, and sword— and went back to farming.

Consuls With Powers Similar To Kings

Kings were out, but consuls with similar powers were in. Perhaps the appeal lay in the concept that whereas a king was a sole ruler, *two* consuls had to be in office—each with the veto over the other. (The idea of having two heads lasted into the empire period. One thing Western Culture took from Rome was to forget this recipe for strife, which produced more civil wars than civilization.)

Either part or all of the time in the struggling, experimenting republic, the people and the law had at least some say in the appointment and tenure of consuls. Also, the "impeachment" or removal idea appeared.

As time went on, there was a senate of the elite.

Furthermore, there appeared two assemblies, the *curiata* for the tribes, and the *centuriata* for the military.

However, did all this represent the people?
Not really.

The population was separated into two classes: patrician and plebian. The Plebes were kept out of the top by various means including religious barriers. Marriage with patricians was forbidden along with any other steps for moving up in society or government.

In time this stark separation was modified. Something called the Tribunate of the Plebes established an elective office for tribunes, and soon these wielded great power, including the veto over practically anyone else's proposals or enactments. The right to intermarry with patrician class people was gained, further breaking down class walls.

By 287, the plebian assembly had the right to pass laws. However, note that this is more than 220 years after the founding of the republic.

The republic was an important historical effort at learning how a government by the people might and might not work. But beyond that, it was two things only: rule from the top, and a great deal of confusion and division when not ruled from the top.

Rome's Expansion From A Mere Town To Control Of A Vast Area Outside Italy

Rome first became a power in central Italy by defeating its neighbors. But further expansion was set back when, around 390 B.C., invading Barbarian Gauls sacked the city.

Recovering, Rome advanced against the Samnites in the north (293 B.C.) and the Greeks in the foot, defeating Pyrrhus on the third try (275). In the Punic or Phoenician Wars with Carthage, Rome won at sea, captured Sicily.

Carthage's famed Hannibal then crossed the Alps. In fifteen years of roaming Italy, he never took the city on the

Tiber. Rome attacked Carthage, Hannibal returned home to lose at Zama in 202.

Thus the 200s B.C. (for a "quick handle") was Rome's consolidation period. She owned Italy, Sicily, Sardinia and Corsica—all under the republic.

In the 100s B.C., she successfully ventured into Macedonia, Syria, Spain, and today's Tunisia, where she defeated Carthage forever in the Third Punic War, leveled the city and "sowed salt in the fields," in 146 B.C.

During This Expansion, How Fared The Republic?

Social and political life was in its usual upheaval. Two new groups constituted the top and bottom—the *optimates* and the *populares*. The optimates were conservative, while the populares were liberal....

So what else is new?

The *equestrians* were a class somewhere in the middle, wooed by both.

Any man could hold office, but in practice the aristocracy still ruled. Since there was no pay, only the rich could afford to serve!

The Decline And Fall Of The...
Republic—*Taken Over By The Empire*

There are various dates for the end of the republic and beginning of the empire.

One is 49 B.C. when the civil wars broke out, described in part below. Another is 31 B.C. when Anthony's sea defeat at Actium put Octavian (who later took the name Augustus

Caesar) into sole control of the internally-torn Rome. The date I use for the purposes of this book is 27 B.C. when Octavian was formally installed as emperor.

The republic actually had failed *long before*, and existed in name only. Listed below are some attempts to reorganize the republic, clearly indicating its collapsed state more than 100 years before its official demise.

The brothers Tiberias and Gaius Gracchus, starting in 134 B.C., each tried land reform (since the land was all owned by the rich). Each led large followings, and was killed.

After them rose Marius—effective for a time before submerging. Drusus followed, making suggestions which got him assassinated. Sulla and Marius then contested top vs. bottom. Sulla eventually prevailed, becoming a dictator before dying in 78 B.C.

A dictator, you say? Again, where's the republic? It ain't—not the way we think it was.

Enter Julius Caesar

Pompey, Caesar and Crassus soon unofficially split things as the "First Triumvirate," having near-total influence but not recognized control.

Crassus (who had put down Spartacus in 71 B.C.) was later killed in war in 53 B.C. After that, Pompey and Caesar became opponents, the former taking control of the Senate and "optimates," while Caesar's following was among the people's "populares."

The Senate ordered Caesar, who was in the north of Italy, to disband his army, but the leader headed south to the border of his control area—the Rubicon.

Which river—recite after me, class—he crossed.

Pompey fled, losing battles to Caesar, winding up in Egypt where he was killed by the Egyptians.

This left Caesar the sole ruler—in fact, dictator for life (some say it was only a ten-year appointment in 46 B.C.). The term mattered little, because, after ruling for only two years, he was assassinated in 44 B.C.

"Chaos"

Where's that republic? Long departed, except in name.

In the period of ninety years from 134 B.C. until that 44 B.C. date (and later), rule was by expediency, graft, and military power.

"Chaos," one source puts it.

Following Caesar's death, Octavian, Anthony, and Lepidus formed the "Second Triumvirate"—Octavian ruling in the West, Anthony in the East, and Lepidus in Africa.

By 36 B.C., Octavian took over in Africa. Anthony fell into Cleo's arms. After the disastrous Battle of Actium in 31 B.C. both Anthony and Cleo committed suicide.

Wrapping Up The Republic

Whereas the republic period showed many examples of pluck, vigorous experimentation with different ideas, and attempts to translate some very good *ideals* into practice, in fact the republic was essentially "business as usual."

While reference books show complete rosters of emperors, they don't list the heads of the ill-fated republic.

Rome's "glory" was tied to its empire, but a romanticized sense of the republic was and is often invoked to give the blood-soaked empire some sense of dignity.

The Empire—Called The Republic

The first emperor, Octavian, said in his opening speech that the *republic* was restored.

The word and ideal had magic even then—just as it apparently still has magic today.

The empire retained some elements of the republic.

For example, the senate still passed laws, although the questions continued to be such things as whether the law-making body represented the people and whether the laws governed, or governed only when convenient.

Up To Its Fall, What Was Rome's Proportion Of Minuses To Pluses?

The minuses far outweighed and outnumbered the pluses, although some periods and regimes might have been even-steven.

Ancient Rome—Uncivil Civilization

Rome can't qualify as the main basis of our modern *civil*ization because its aggression and most of its existence were too *un*civil. It didn't last because it couldn't last.

-

CODA:
Was The Church After A.D. 476
An Extension Of The Western Roman Empire?

The Church at Rome became extremely powerful and deeply involved with the governments of nations well into recent times.

Did this make it an extension of the Roman Empire?

Or perhaps an empire in itself?

Or was it an umbrella, much as Islam is the umbrella power over many governments although not technically governing?

Or maybe a little of all of these?

I've read and not believed treatises presenting the Catholic Church as the Book of Revelation's "great red dragon," and "Babylonian woman" "sitting on" or controlling the minds of peoples, nations, tongues and kings (see Rev. 18).

If true, the Church could be the big, bad, final empire.

Personally, I don't agree with such concepts.

I admire the dedication of many of its people, and can't believe its destiny is anything but good.

Will its spirit change after John Paul II and one other pope depart, as Malachy's prophecies say? I don't know.

The Church once got deeply into exercising a governing influence over other governments, and certainly over people's minds. This, however, has receded.

As a prominent Catholic commented on TV recently regarding some abuses in the deep past, "We were in the governing business then, but not now."

In its governing days, the Church could be "heavy."
TIME-LIFE's *Great Ages of Man—Imperial Rome* says that before the fall of Rome, the Church was itself exercising power almost like emperors, and executing heretics.

After the fall of Rome, the Church continued to assume powers, size and authority, expanding for many centuries and becoming a major factor in Western Civilization.

It became involved in monarchies, wars between nations or principalities, oppression of science, torture and deaths of heretics, infidels, Jews and "secret Jews," mind-control, thought-control, expression-control, religion-control epitomized in its inquisitions (lasting for centuries but particularly identified with Torquemada in Spain in the late 1400s), and wars with Protestants.

Were Inquisitions defending religious purity, or the concept of absolute rule from the top?

Interesting in this context is a statement from *Ecclesia Militans—The Inquisition,* attributed to Gabriel Naude way back then, that "In Rome, they forgive atheists, sodomites, libertines and all other kinds of offenders, but they will never forgive anyone who speaks badly of the pope or of the curia or who even creates an impression of having doubts about papal omnipotence."

A Magnificent Step Indicates
The Church Isn't Returning To
Unwanted Governing Of Others

Vatican II in the 1960s declared religious freedom for all—no more persecutions of other religions. This was a very progressive step, showing great stature and boding well for the broad body of Christianity.

I think we can expect the best—not the worst—to come from the Catholics.

Divine healing is now permitted, practiced by Cathoolic Pentecostals and Catholic Charismatics, and ministered in some churches by priests.

Will part of the Church spiritualize? Definitely, just as Jacob changed (which is the theme of this book).

Will part secularize? It's possible; no one knows.

If such separation occurs, will the secularizing part join the end-time empire prophesied as "not yet come"? That's possible; again, no one knows.

The same influences of secularization and spiritualization will also affect other Christian denominations, but those are not watched as closely because they have not had the near-empire status of the Roman Catholic Church.

< >

10
THE FINAL EMPIRE—VII—"NOT YET COME"

Will The Seventh Biblical Empire
Rise In The Last Days To Challenge
The Coming Kingdom?

"Five are fallen, and one is, and the other is not yet come." So wrote John in Revelation (17:10). In addition to the "one not yet come," Revelation also tells us of a last-days empire under "666." Are these two the same? Probably.

Revelation reveals climaxes which subordinate evil to divine power on earth before the final end of evil itself.

Since the devil will be in the earth knowing he hath but a "short time" (Rev. 12:9, 12), it's logical that evil will seek strength by uniting in one empire. I expect the ancient bad spirits—still busy though their empires fell—to gather there to oppose the divine Kingdom coming on earth.

Many interpreters believe the EU will become a "revived Roman Empire" and the seventh opponent.

It's The "End Of The Age"—The Age In Which
Any Sense Of "Israel" Can Be Defeated

A new age is emerging, an old one passing. This is a "rolling" event, taking place even now. It will probably have several sub-climaxes before the big one.

The gathering of evil into one entity or coalition occurs in reaction to the coming Kingdom, perceived by evil as a threat to its very existence. However, when concentrated, evil is exposed, making its destruction easier, not harder. In panic, it may appear more terrible than ever for a time.

There are three senses of "Israel": the Jacob change, the Israelite people, and the land of Israel (first, the northern kingdom of David; today, the nation of Israel).

Each of the ancient empires defeated Israel in the sense of the people and in the sense of the land. Rome dealt the Jacob-change "Israel" a death blow, consigning it to a long period of "night" prior to its resurrection in these end times.

The fact of the reappearance of divine healing in a knowledgeable, certain and broad way that cannot be overthrown this time is the camel's nose under the tent that will lead to evil's demise, not healing's demise as before.

By appearing more threatening than ever, evil will try to scare or discourage us; however, spiritual warriors will grow in numbers and strength as they perceive the divine Kingdom "at hand" and their spiritual identity. They will change, grow, and gain confidence from successful exercise of biblical overcoming —from experience in battle.

Evil cannot win the fight this time, although it may win some rounds. The great deceiver will lose.

The Antichrist?

Will the last empire be headed by "The Antichrist"?

"The Antichrist" is an oft-used term today, yet John said "even now are there many antichrists" (I Jn. 2:18).

"*The* Antichrist" isn't a term in my Bible concordance; therefore it could be a force, not a man, working through many individuals and power structures in history.

Around us today we can see both forces and people "anti" to Christ— just as in the early times.

Nevertheless, I can accept the position of many interpreters, that a single most extreme example may appear.

Rome was opposed to Jesus. That's "anti."

The mass of Jews, who liked Jesus, were not to blame for his death. However, there was anti-Jesus input at his trial from Caiaphas, the secularized chief priest who, although Jewish, presented a *reverse of* Abraham's Judaism. Rome went along, and at the end, carried out the deed.

The Judaic structure of the time (exemplified by Caiaphas), opposed Jesus, fearing a "king of the Jews." Jesus' power to heal and change, plus prophecy, plus his popularity with the ordinary Jews, made him a threat to the priestly structure.

Both Rome and the priests felt the rebuke of the representative of the divine kingdom. Would God's kingdom come on earth? Not if they could prevent it.

All this is "anti."

Rome then bitterly attacked the disturbing *Christians*, their power-Christianity and preaching of a new kingdom.

Man's "Kingdom, Power And Glory"

The "Rome" concept presents *man's* kingdom, power and glory—the direct opposite of the divine kingdom.

In The "Latter Days, "
Evil's Power Is Thrown Into The Pit

We're already in the "latter days. "

After the physical and mental battle climaxes defeating evil by divine power, evil will be in the inferior position and size. It never will have the upper hand again, and we will know clearly how to embody and use our upper hand.

The Scriptures refer to evil as coming from the "bottomless pit" (for instance, Rev. 11:7, which describes the "beast" coming out to kill the two "witnesses").

This sounds scary but in my opinion merely means that evil has no foundation—that God fills depths and heights. The devil's shift from "heaven" to "earth" (Rev. 12:7-12) shows it has no place in heaven, while the "bottomless pit" shows the devil has no footing in an earth-pit either.

The Millennium

The start of the millennium doesn't mark the end of evil, just the *control* of evil. The devil—defeated and *returned* to the bottomless pit (Rev. 20:1-3)—comes out at the *end* for a final fling, which is brief, and weak.

Throughout the 1,000 years, there will be the "multitudes in the valley of decision, " struggling with themselves.

When Can We Expect These Things?

They're well underway, but the empire (or coalition) hasn't appeared yet, and we haven't reached any climaxes.

Events aren't tied to any particular year, because they depend so much on the breakthroughs whereby we obtain change, and on our subsequent victories.

Jesus said no man knew the time, yet he told us of many *signs* of the times so we could be alert (see Mat. 24).

Making the matter of *time* even more obscure for today's interpreters, scholars argue differences in prophetic time frameworks ranging up to seven years B.C. in the birth of Jesus, and discuss whether prophecies hinge on his birth date or the Cross and Resurrection, or standard chronology such as the year 2000.

Thus, the timeline isn't clear.

Even while trying to pin down the times for prophetic fulfillments, scholars remind us that Jesus said only the Father, not man, knew the time (Mat. 24:36).

I interpret Jesus' words to mean that the Father knows that when we wake up to Him, that's what changes things.

Scholars also remind us that once the prophesied hell breaks loose, the times will be "shortened" for the "elect's sake" (Mat. 24:22).

I interpret that to mean that the "elect" so utterly break through to the ever-present divine kingdom of good that they put an end to the carnal mind's murdering. The alternate interpretation is that "the elect" are pitied by God, so He quits killing everyone in sight, to preserve the elect.

The "Fig Tree" And The "Generation"

In the quote where Jesus gives us an approximate date of the end, he said, "Now learn a parable of the fig tree; When his branch is yet tender, and putteth forth leaves, ye know that summer is nigh: So likewise ye, when ye shall see all these things, know that it is near, even at the doors. Verily I say unto you, This generation shall not pass, till all these things be fulfilled" (Mat. 24:32-34.)

What's the "fig tree" and its "leaves," and what's the "generation" that will see the divine kingdom come?

Many have concluded that the "fig tree" putting forth "leaves" is the establishment of the Jewish nation in 1948. Trying to fit prophecies to this basing point, interpreters have used twenty, thirty, forty, and now fifty years for "a generation."

However, is the term "generation" ever used scripturally in a context other than human generations? (We know it's used for human generations, as in the extensive Bible "begats," but does it ever have another meaning?)

Yes. Of the good guys, the Bible says, "Ye are a chosen generation...an holy nation, a peculiar people; that ye should shew forth the praises of him who hath called you out of darkness into his marvelous light: Which...are now the people of God" (I Pet. 2:9-10).

And Jesus referred to bad guys as a "generation of vipers," a "wicked generation," a "perverse generation."

These references are to a group or type, not to a specific human generation or number of years such as twenty.

As I see it then, "This generation" that sees the fig tree and its leaves is a group which holds a particular awareness.

*"The Leaves Of The Tree Are For The
Healing Of The Nations" (Rev. 22:2)*

If we use the reappearance of divine healing, which is a restoration of one of our meanings of "Israel," for Jesus' "fig tree" that "putteth forth leaves," this doesn't divorce us from the founding of the nation, which is another of our meanings of Israel.

The founding of the nation is itself is a type of healing—as are its many evidences such as the desert blooming and other prophesied things (appearing in the manner that healing appears: from the progressive revelation of unseen spiritual Creation as in Jacob's change to Israel).

The "generation" that sees this fig leaf will see—and currently sees part of—the Kingdom coming "on earth."

As it sees more of this Kingdom, more changes will result.

*Why Only Seven Empires—
When There Were Plenty More Big, Bad Ones?*

There've been many bloody empires since the German tribes extinguished the western Roman Empire A.D. 476.

Wasn't Genghis Khan and his dynasty of warlords which entered Europe from Mongolia, an empire? Yes.

Or Napoleon, Hitler's "second reich"? Surely.

Or Hitler's vast "Third Reich"—*particularly since it so especially persecuted Jews?* Absolutely.

What of Russia's former Communist Empire? Certainly. (And Russia is biblically predicted to attack Israel.)

The unifying thread of the oldies is that they conquered the Jewish homeland or, in the case of ancient Egypt, enslaved and persecuted the Hebrew population.

What could the latecomer empires add to the inventory of evils? Nothing that wasn't already represented by an ancient empire.

(Hitler, however, is reminiscent of the ancients because of his vicious attack on Jews. Whereas the Nazi empire wasn't the seventh, I think it was a forerunner. Consider that if world war is the "red horse" or second horseman or "war" horse of the Apocalypse, which, along with false peace, famine, and pestilence, "ride to the end"— a concept of the four horsemen put forth by Tom Linder in his *Timetable of Bible Prophecy*—then World War II prefaced the end-time, and anti-Israel will be a part of the *final* empire and war.)

The Final Empire Is Distinguished By Its
Involvement With Science And The Scientific Age

The final empire rises in the scientific age. In my opinion, it will present both a primitive roar and the most advanced state of sciences evil and good, old and new, invisible and visible, inside us and outside, mental and physical, religious-seeming and secular, in history. Deceit (the devil's a liar) will be the cleverest science, making more traps than ever appear good. Illusion will rise to new heights of hypnotic, convincing power.

Maybe the final empire awaits one more electronic revolution (next week?) to put astonishing powers in its hands.

In the past, high-tech was for *consumer* markets, to make money. The geniuses were "good guys" (so to speak).

The next wave of inventions might come from the minds of "bad guys" appearing sweet but wanting *control*.

Revelation Mentions An Eighth Empire — And Maybe Others—But Only Faintly

"The beast that was, and is not, even he is the eighth," we learn in Rev. 17:10-12. However, the passages quickly add that he is "of the seven," and "goeth into perdition." So I think the eighth is just an offshoot "of the seven."

Revelation mentions "ten kings" who have no kingdom but "received power as kings one hour with the beast."

These could be powerful leaders within the final empire, in that they "have no kingdom" of their own, apparently, but have power only with the "beast" which may be the final empire.

The Identity Of "666"—If Indeed He, She, Or It Heads The Final Empire

To the widespread speculation about the identity of "666," I've earlier added my concept that this "man" may be the "legal person" of the corporation—not a flesh and blood man or woman at all. And this would fit in well with the commercial/ corporate scenario, even the EU.

Maybe 666 is a *super-computer.* Maybe the empire is cyber, the image of the beast, or even 666, a *cyber-person.*

The Bible's statement that "all" must have a "mark" in the head or hand in order to "buy or sell" wouldn't seem strange in such a world of high-tech. (Note however, that "names...written in the book of life" are excepted.)

-

Yeah?

In a super-technocracy (or world empire) of rule by technical things and people, the electronics needed for all transactions of any kind would be utterly controlled by the people who designed and manufactured the systems and software (along with its "scrubbers" to destroy all other systems), and who knew how to maintain and upgrade these.

The forerunner of such a technocracy is already steadily coming into place, and each ongoing change puts everything farther and farther out of reach of the average person.

After multiple further mergers of corporations, the final remaining electronics super-corporation will be the government. The military, helpless without the latest electronics, will be taught only what it needs to know. (World War II's apex of high-tech—the cracking of the German code—was controlled by the British government. Today's high-tech runs our government and military.)

The new system will issue tax notices, confiscate your houses—and do all the other things the IRS used to do.

As for you—you museum-piece "voter," you—you can't even fix your vacuum cleaner, so you'll function the way they tell you to function, jump when they say jump.

And if you're not connected to the new system (and don't think you can hide—they *know* who you are, and where you are) you'll get a midnight knock on the door....

I say this with a smile, but maybe it ain't a joking matter.

< >

11
DOUBLE TROUBLE IN THE END-TIME

Double Power Brings Double Reaction

We're already in the foothills of "double power" to overcome evil. Evil's response will be "double."

Spiritual Climbing Forces Evil Into The Open

Ineffective as we may think we are, if we're spiritually climbing, evil has to match us. Thus our efforts draw it from hiding where it can be dissolved by divine light.

Ultimately, all evil will disappear because it isn't in God, and God is coming to our benighted thought in proportion to our use of divine light. Soon the "earth shall be filled with the knowledge of the glory of the Lord, as the waters cover the sea" (Hab. 2:14).

Spiritual warriors occupy ground. This is "double" hard work. It often appears to be losing, but it isn't.

Today's "Double Death" Spike Lurks And Jabs

The sword of Damocles hung over the king's head, suspended by only a hair.

The "spike" of death has hung over all humans from the mortal beginning, hiding in the murk and thrusting in the open, limiting and intimidating in myriad ways.

As double power comes in the end times, "double death" responds.

It attempts two things: to continue its claim to be the ultimate power; and to blame the end-time destruction on God.

The "Last Enemy" To Be Overcome Is Death (I Cor. 15:26)

The carnal mind (Rom. 8:6) not God, has (and is) death, and we must learn how to overcome this last enemy, which Jesus overcame first.

Will we raise the dead tomorrow with our present, elementary-school level of Christian power? It isn't likely, although beginners sometimes have such a pure sense that remarkable things happen; and we mustn't limit God, who can show us His power anytime we're open to it. At the same time, though, Scripture tells us of progress by steps.

Heart Of Darkness, Heart Of Light

Is God unchanging light, "with whom is no variableness, neither shadow of turning" (James 1:17)? And was

John right, that "God is light, and in him is no darkness at all" (I Jn. 1:5)?

Yes, and this "heart of light" is the key to divine over-coming. Evil as darkness cannot stand in its presence.

Is God waiting for the moment to crush evil with an even more terrible smashing and killing power He has in reserve? Even if termed "good," this would nonetheless mean we'd never be rid of evil.

Is He waiting to finally crush all unrepentant sinners — *splat*? No, He redeems all sinners, even if the early stages are a rough experience like the ore-smelting in Malachi, brought about by progressive awareness of our higher being in His image as in Genesis 1.

It's pure divine goodness, not splat power, that eliminates evil.

One great miracle is that God leads us up by steps, not imputing sins (II Cor. 5:19) but helping us shed sins and, particularly, find the new life He's revealing for us, which gradually replaces the old without harm.

Human goodness may be weaker than evil, but divine good is all-powerful. If our personal goodness gets beaten up by evil, the divine is another dimension, and wins.

The Heavy Emphasis On Death Seen Today
Is The End-Time Double Death At Work Trying
To Convince Us It's The Ultimate Power

Our movies today feature destruction on a scale un-imagined a few years ago—entire cities blowing up, super-twisters and horrific volcanoes raging, ships sinking.

Theme park shows feature more of the same. Terminators, thousands of bodies.

Mega death type video games and posters are absorbed by many in a variety and intensity non-users wouldn't believe.

Armageddon world-annihilation concepts from books, movies and pulpits have people fearing fast or slow death by nukes, radiation clouds, disease epidemics, and so on.

Read these things: "double death" asserting itself.

Using The Double Christian Power—
Awareness Of God's Kingdom
And Man's Higher Identity—
Spiritual Warriors Advance,
But Like The Seesaw Toy Climbing The Pole

We climb, then are set back.

It's important to rally when we're set back, then climb again. And "repeat the process."

In our setbacks, we never go as deep as we were before, although it may seem deeper. Then we notch upward again.

Often the message on the humorous plaque is true, "No good deed shall go unpunished."

Blows received in opposition to your spiritual progress are just opportunities to climb again, get into a higher range of power and performance.

Sometimes the light we encounter reveals a dark abyss "beneath our floorboards."

· This can be really discouraging, when instead it gives us the opportunity to see the work we still have to do within ourselves.

As mentioned earlier, we mustn't kill our lower natures but minister to them as long as they're part of ourselves and not "devils"—letting the pattern of the parable of the wheat and the tares be our guide.

Evil's Great Wonders

Evil will produce great wonders designed to fool even the "elect" (Mat. 24:24), frighten many whose hearts will fail them (Lk. 21:26), and murder one-third of the world's population on a single occasion or war (Rev. 9:18).

Evil will say God did it, in order to deflect blame from itself, and in order to make humans feel incapable of defending themselves if the hell is coming from God.

Society Isn't Yet In An Overcoming Mode— In Fact, It's "Dancin'" To Avoid The Spike

In the old cowboy movie, the villain fired bullets so they bounced off the road surface or flew off the floor of the saloon, and told the victim to "dance!"

The double-reaction spike jabbing from all sides has already started populations "dancin'."

We Fear Being Stationary

We fear being stationary, lest we be pinned down.

We rush to and fro, this kinetic action affirming life.

However, this immense activity isn't saving us. We're merely reacting more ineffectively than before to the now-doubled death threats of the end times.

The Frantic Society—"To And Fro"

Spectator games seem to affirm life, and by *keeping things moving* for us, vicariously prevent us from being pinned down.

The games we literally worship today are mostly "to and fro" contests, desperately surging between "goals" or back and forth over nets for... *hours*.

Into games, entertainment, and other things, the people invest their psyches. It's a vicarious transfer by which identity is found inside this secondary ambience.

We pay our "champions" incredible sums, make them gods, and speak of "immortality" over some...stat.

However, this only postpones the development of the individual, when instead what's needed is growth and competence to handle the end-time situation.

Males have always reacted strongly, even heroically, to passivating forces—building great exterior appearances, making money, racking up female "conquests," defeating competition, going to war, talking big.

The most passivating, threatening force for everyone has always been the spike in many seen and unseen forms.

Reaction supposedly proves people don't have a vulnerable center threatened by internal and external, visible and invisible, single and multidirectional jabbings.

In the end-time, since the spike is doubled, reactions will be greater in magnitude.

Actually, real life will be obtained not by the great things produced in *reaction to* the spike's many minor and major forms, but by *overcoming* it.

Bouncing Off The Walls

The carnal mind is a "kingdom divided." Its innate dichotomy nature blows our minds and keeps us from "getting our minds around the outside of it."

Paradoxes causing minds to zip like alternating current from one wall of our consciousness to the other include the original "no-no" and "yes-yes" of the Garden of Eden on the most important thing to the human flesh: sex.
The even more basic dichotomy is "mortal life."

We're "bouncing off walls"; our minds cannot settle on any one side, also cannot stop anywhere on the inside lest we get penetrated.
We can't escape without divine revelation of a better total system, and major restructuring of our consciousness.

How Do We Defeat Evil?

Individuals must seek. Even though most answers keep us within the death framework, we must seek higher.
The answers exist. When an individual finds the answers, he or she still can't just walk off. Progress is by steps of overcoming internally and externally.
Jesus said we must "heal the sick, cleanse the lepers, raise the dead, cast out devils" (Mat. 10:8), and do the works that he did (Jn. 14:12).
Overcoming is necessary before the "end"—of evil.

< >

12
CLUTTER BLOCKS NECESSARY CHANGE

Abraham And TV?

If Abraham had been subjected to TV shows, commercials, pounding sound tracks....

If he had been exposed to sports with their gladiatorial pyramidal-elimination Athens-Sparta city-state team wars (with media overhype)....

If he had been impressed by stars....

If he had been able to buy bumper sticker logos for his donkeys and "gear" for his tent....

If he had lost himself in vicarious entertainment....

If he had adopted a commercially-furnished "identity" for himself....

Would he ever have heard God's instructions to go to "a land that I will shew thee" (Gen. 12:1)? Or would he ever have had the higher experiences which led to his and Sarah's change and Isaac's birth in their very old age (Gen. 17-21)?

Probably not.

The Mortal Realm's "Game Plan"

For the "world" (I Jn. 2:15-17; Jn. 16:33) to remain in control, it must stop people from spiritually advancing.

By occupying the human senses with hypnotic sounds, pictures, and glorification of things not worthy of glorification, people won't seek or perceive higher things; hence won't spiritually advance.

Weapons Of "Mass Distraction"

Today, the former fortresses of our beliefs are overrun by dozens of perspectives, lifestyles, and thought systems (or simply by chaos: the lack of systems). Even the unworthy and trivial are often presented by celebrities and accompanied by trumpets, percussion, spotlights, glitter, applause, and super-publicity to impress us. Our attention is grabbed and held.

Our perception of the higher realm—which perception and resultant change and empowerment spells evil's eventual doom—is postponed when our senses can be fixated on attractions and fascinations the opposite of the burning bush.

"Homogenization"

Good and evil, purity and dirt, clarity and obscurity, honesty and dishonesty, high and low, are so mingled in our culture today that we scarcely make differentiations any more. We're in the age of accommodation of all concepts, lifestyles, and beliefs.

If we adopt a standpoint outside of this "graysville," we are out of the mainstream—even called extreme; and very likely then to be shut out.

Right and wrong are so blended in our society, that we seem to believe—and can even argue—both sides.

Remember The Old Cowboy Films?

Once there was something called the "morality play" (for example, the old-time cowboy movie) with clear-cut good and evil resulting in victory for the good and punishment for the evil.

Despite once being central to US culture, the "morality play" has almost vanished.

Weren't God and mammon once opposites? Today, preachers amass huge amounts of money.

Politicians want to be our leaders, but from the outset they break both the Golden Rule and the commandment about bearing false witness against their opponent—then "win" that seat.

Things that once dwelt in the shadows of our thoughts and behavior are today accepted in the daylight.

Never before this hour have we had the dark side so thoroughly set up as "belonging"—or even celebritized as on so many TV shows.

Voices Of Differentiation Gone

The great voices of differentiation—the 1950s parent, teacher, newspaper editor, school principal, preacher, hardware store owner rising at the town meeting—aren't heard, or if heard, aren't followed. Instead, we hear and see televised dramas with their vast mixture of "homogenized," undifferentiated concepts.

Entertained By Evil

If tuned to a popular TV talk and celebrity show, we might hear, "Now we'll enter the gang world, and meet some of the people, including Quick Nick sitting here, who admits to participating in five drive-by shootings, some of which resulted in deaths. Nick, tell the audience, what was it like, and what made you do these things?"

On the particular show I watched, "Nick" denied, under questioning by the audience (which had been titillated to believe he was a killer), that he personally shot anyone.

However, throwing bullets out there, who knows who shot whom?

We're "entertained" by some disguised cat who runs a produce market and also goes out of town weekends as a hit man. Or by some judge who was highly respected except that he beat up women in a lower life, and is doing the TV talk show tour to sell his book-apologia about it all.

Celebrity Status For Anything And Everything

The big voice of celebrity TV with its stars, pounding sound tracks, lights, and rabidly-clapping audiences, creates a situation where we're being told that anything we're watching is normal and acceptable, and furthermore, *worthy of celebrity status.*

Does Evil Have "Rights"?

Under some kind of "no discrimination" concept, we refuse to eliminate evil; after all, it has its rights. But does it?

Evil is set up three different ways today: as equal; as worthy of blending in as part of our scene; as superior, ultimate, and inevitable.

Murder And Destruction Entertainment Thrills

We can't get enough murder and destruction entertainment, and I'll explain later below how an addiction to this is steadily advancing its grip.

Explosions—Fascinating If Fake, Horrifying If Real

It's interesting that we can be excited by violent, fiery, screen explosions. A little friend beside me in the movies jumped up and said, "Wow!" as a blast destroyed a car.

The fake may seem exciting, but in real fires (many with secondary explosions from chemicals, paints, gas or gasoline, and where glass shards and metal fragments are flying) people die, their faces are slashed, and their skin is melted.

On local TV news, if even a small fire or blast occurs, it's considered deadly, not exciting, and may get close-ups of bandages and weeping relatives of the injured or lost.

From this we can see there's a large gap between our gluttonous appetites in the imagination, and our cringing aversion to real fires, car wrecks, and so on.

"Hey, That's Fantastic! Look At That!"

When the Italians invaded Ethiopia in World War II, there was a story about their bombing from 10,000 feet. This was described as comfortable, and even pretty, as the white puffs from the detonations spread out so far below. It was antiseptic warfare: one didn't have to get one's hands dirty, risk one's neck (the enemy possessed spears), or witness the death and dismemberment of men, women and children, disruption of food and water supplies, and so on.

Today we watch the White House blown up in a TV movie and say, "Hey, that's fantastic! Look at that!"

The Trend Is To Ever-Increasing Quantities Of Murder And Destruction Entertainment Because Last Week's Levels Won't "Do It" For Us Anymore

Where one killing, horrible accident or incident per show formerly sufficed, now we need continuous slaughter and shock from start to finish.

One fiery explosion used to titillate. Now we need to witness the destruction of entire cities.

What We're Experiencing Is Increasing Addiction To Painkilling Drugs In Our Own Brains

Once we went to campy "horror shows" where we insulated our psyches by keeping the gruesomeness "compartmentalized" at a sort of arm's length with lots of laughing and popcorn. Now horror gets to our brains.

When faced with genuine shock, the brain assuages itself with its own painkillers.

These are addictive, leading the individual to seek repetition of the shock in order to obtain the drug.

Worse, as with all drugs, the dosage has to be stepped up slightly or more to obtain the same fix as before.

Hence, the steadily-increasing quantities and intensities of murder and destruction "entertainment."

The Overstatement Phenomenon

Films and TV today take any problem and overstate it ten times. Twisters were bad enough without *Twister*.

These titillate us at the moment but result in numbness later. Real twisters, serial killers and rapists seem less astonishing, dangerous, and so on, than the movie ones.

Creeping Brain-drug Addiction

We know that adrenaline can produce forms of addiction, which explains why some people *need* harrowing action and anxiety.

We've also heard that in the compulsive gambling syndrome, the gambler is addicted to losing, and will play to lose in order to obtain the pain and ignominy which in turn is assuaged by the drugs secreted by his brain. Later, he must lose again in order to get this fix.

Doctors appearing on TV talk shows have shown that some women complaining of going from one abusive mate to another, and then another, were hooked on a repetition of disaster, the blame laid on addictive pain-assuaging brain chemicals.

Sexualization Of Shock

Torture in prisons is said to sometimes cause "Stockholm Syndrome," where the abusee "loves" the abuser.

This is Freud's "sensualization," "pleasurization," or plain "libidinization" (sexualization) of the pain, humiliation, degradation, fear, oppression, or whatever.

Today we know this state is aided or directly produced by self-secreted pain assuagers—internally generated and administered mental drugs.

(The term "Stockholm Syndrome" has been used for everything from diaper rash to baldness, but its original and only meaning is stated above.)

We "love" our shocks—but do we really love them, or do we love getting our secret pain killers?

We can also become addicted to positive things such as the stock market going up. The big mutual funds committing more and more money make it go up. There's an excitement and a blaze from brain synapses that "begs" for another and another such experience.

Or if a loss of confidence breaks the lockstep—or if people quit backing the action by pouring in money— investors can always switch back and get something from shock, misery and losing again.

Gods And Goddesses Are More Obstructive Clutter

The US today has more mythological gods and goddesses, human and invented, including heroes and the new category of "super-heroes" ("double heroes"), than all the nations in history put together—but we don't realize it.

We have endless human idols and heroes in sports, entertainment and the new category of business and finance.

We have our cartoon heroes and "super-heroes" animal and human—totally mythological.

We worship Eros. In diversity of erotic aspects including "telephone sex," and in sheer numbers of participants, we exceed anything previously seen in history.

And then there's the goddess of fortune. We've given ourselves to her instead of seeking to our God, and without realizing that the sinister fellow barely seen behind her shining robes and beckoning smile is the devil of misfortune. The two are really one, and inseparable.

"I have declared, and have saved, and I have shewed, when there was no strange god among you...saith the Lord" (Isa. 43:12).

Cartoons And Costumes

Many so-called super-identities in the US are but cartoon humans or animals—or a little of both—existing only in our minds and possessing only the actions and powers over evil (or evil powers) that we attribute to them as they soar, "win," go "POW!", "SOCK!", and so forth.

Many are portrayed in films by popular actor-stars, further blurring the lines of distinction.

Spiderman. Batman. Superman. Turtles. And so on.

We tell our children there's no Santa Claus but say, "Oh, look—there's Mickey!" Folks, there is no Mickey Mouse.

There's no Barney. Why feed our children this pap?

Now Big Bird—Big Bird is *real*.

Adults Gobble Fairy Tales

Once, the age range for which TV and movies were produced was roughly thirteen to twenty-seven. That left older adults hungry. But they adjusted to lower levels when publicity from serious news media reassured them that something important, funny, or worthy of their time and attention was taking place.

But now the adults are down to the nine-year-old range—my age when I last had an interest in Batman (then appearing in comic books only). Today's *news* editors flack Batman and similar material shamelessly, and "film critics" rave.

Continuing the "age slide," we keep presenting new dramatizations of children's fairy tales (crib and up), expanding them with music and theater arts magic, and marketing them to enthralled adults.

Hey, our minds could be softening. If not, then at least agree with me that we're no longer occupying our minds wrestling with great problems.

We're asleep—or at the least, thoroughly lulled.

Free Publicity

How does the entertainment industry get its free publicity into serious newscasts? By finding an angle such as "How those special effects were done." Or, "Eighty-eight million pieces of animation art—a new record!" Interesting but hardly important, these get on "20/20" or "Prime Time Live!" in free ten-minute "segments" going out to millions under the aegis of serious reporting.

I'd like to "meet" the stuntperson if *well after thc ̖ ͤͤͥ—* when it's not a bald, unpaid promo for a movie. But once I know it's a disguised ad for a show mixed in with the serious news, I change channels.

There's a brand-new "news" category the flack artists have created—"Weekend box-office receipts." Not only is this "vital statistic" published with a straight face as "news" but "news stories" based on this "news" are run.
It's all promotional stuff, coinciding with the release.

Without an apology, a big newspaper in 1997 ran on its *front page*, as a three-column *news story*—not in one of those "skyboxes" above the masthead, or "sidebars" with miscellaneous tidbits —that such and such film was going to be tied in with a *popular hamburger chain!* Yes folks! And little dolls would be available! And printed cups given away!
That's a front page news story, certainly.
In fact, it probably shouldn't qualify even for the "Entertainment" section, except under a catch-all column of incidental news.

"Cultural Icons" Are...News?

One hard-nosed network evening news editor-anchor plainly told his audience he would report, as news, happenings involving American "cultural icons," two of which are Mickey and Elvis.
We all know that if the US president did something that day, he would qualify for a *news* mention.
But now, if Mickey, or Elvis' PPP (Posthumous Publicity Persona), did something, this would *also* qualify because the figure has become "real": a "cultural icon."

That is, a mythological god.

In that atmosphere, busy publicists grind out "icon news" tied to any peg. Anniversaries such as this or that platinum record, the first big tour of Madagascar, the tenth movie, the first T-shirt (a couple of million copies standing by in the stores, of course), and on and on. These are all then given "ink" or "air time" by the serious press.

Elvis makes more money today than when he was alive, due to skillful manipulation of the "news" and publicity by the managers of his estate to keep him in a place in our growing mental panoply where we now demand his presence due to our psychological need.

Elvis is on a postage stamp, but not because the post office was that impressed. Instead, it knows that the engraven images of him will be bought, made part of collections, and therefore stored, not used for postage. Thus, the post office rakes in millions, it admits, for which it will never have to deliver the corresponding amount of mail.

The appearance of the stamp—before, during and after —was reported by the *network evening news* shows. Not long after that, I went to the brand-new post office near me where they have a "store." I was astounded at the displays of dozens of different, absolutely gorgeous stamp offerings —many new—but none had ever been publicized! Hmm.

Elvis is king? He's not my king.

Are We Losing The Line Between Imagination And Reality In This Age Of Illusion?

We've gone unabashedly overboard for "imagination" (instead of "casting down imaginations"—II Cor. 10:5), and for virtual reality and other illusions, losing the line between imagination and reality.

Somewhere in that realm is the overemphasis on sex, "sex fantasies," and finally, "telephone sex fantasies."

The Historic Roles Of King And Entertainer
Have Been Reversed
In Today's Clutter-Filled Lives

Once the entertainer amused the king.

Now the entertainer *is* king.

Our Roman "circuses"—our various entertainments and entertainers—have collectively become a leading industry in the country in the past fifteen years.

Entertainment is an essential part of the plush new company sto' presently encapsulating all (see later below).

"Double Vicarious" Entertainment: "Gotcha!"

Once we went to the movies and identified briefly with the film's story. We were the fighter pilot, or the mother with sixteen children, or the homesteader family in the covered wagon, or the kid with the dog, or whatever. We cried when things were sad, we rejoiced in victories. Then we returned home where we pursued the necessary, traditional search for "Who am I?" and "Why am I here?"

Today, We Stay Inside The Show Permanently

We're in a "double vicarious," or permanent, encapsulation, where we *don't go home,* so to speak, *after the show.*

Instead, we *remain inside* the entertainment realm, getting stardust, excitement, success. We feel we're "really movin'."

The outside is dull by comparison.

An Inside Identity Just For You!

We're outclassed, and we know we're not really a part of the exciting, talented, winning, multiple-screen, star-studded, illusory, money-drenched, lucky, "celebrity" scenario (with all of its lights, trumpets, and publicity).

But take heart! The "inner ambience" is providing us with an "identity" that enables us to fit right into its reality.

Yeah? We *belong?*

Absolutely, as long as we accept one or another of the psychologically-developed, ad-agency-invented and manufactured, lab-tested, scientific, zippy "identities"—even *lifestyles* or *"generations"*—in many models constantly updated or newly-created (one designed with you in mind), to be us, instead of the dull fellow we were born as.

We wear ad logos on our clothing and vehicles—free! (When I was young, "sandwich board" men were *paid* to walk around sidewalks advertising products.)

Replacing weather-talk, we connect conversationally with others via sports events, stars, TV shows, movies or commercials.

For example, if a serious message is to be delivered, it might begin with a reference to Michael in order to "log on" to the minds of listeners.

We pay twelve-fifty for that logo cap which we could buy for three bucks without the badge of identification.

They get the money, we get the "belonging."

Once we've satisfied our psyches, we don't have to live with our dull old untalented selves, or struggle in the tiresome, age-old quest for "Who am I?" and "Why am I here?"

But do we actually get a new life, goals, framework, purpose, and success, or only something skillfully designed to give us a feeling of identification, and keep us in this peppy commercial lockup.

Should The Trusted Media Be Drawing The Crowd For Commercial Interests?

Trumpets and mind-commanding percussion introduce trusted media announcers, reporters or analysts proclaiming an upcoming event, show, or new product—or that victory by Smithtown over Jonesville is "important."

Remember, though, that the media make their living drawing a crowd.

Give me that again?

We don't realize that the powerful, trusted, voice of the collective media has a built-in *bias* to tell us the mediocre is great, the nonessential *vital*.

The larger the crowd, the more can be charged for print ads or electronic commercials. Therefore, *interest must be heightened by all means*.

Every passing of gas by those on stage, court, or in the spotlight must be analyzed, have records kept, statistics archived, awards given, halls of fame erected.

Interest must be riveted, held, institutionalized.

Gee, don't we see this?

When the old medicine shows were the biggest things to hit town, they drew only a few dozen people. The later circuses drew only thousands. By comparison, ordinary TV shows draw millions, the Oscars and Super Bowl a billion, and a syndicated show rerun many times over the years....

The money is hyper-huge today—as long as the crowd is hyper-huge. So it's essential to alert, draw, and hold that crowd. Souls are sold to accomplish this (but sold for big bucks).

Pay TV is in its infancy. Soon we may pay as much via electronic tickets as we presently pay indirectly via commercials bought by advertisers. The inevitability of more pay TV is written in the many millions boxers make from fights. That's giving a lot of producers ideas.

Stars Appear On Talk Shows For Peanuts Because In Exchange They Get Rave Reviews Even For Awful Stuff

Stars make the talk shows successful. The host makes $20 million a year including syndication profits ($100,000 a show for, say, each of 200 shows). Yet the stars who bring all this success are paid *only $200 or so* per appearance.

Since this doesn't make sense, there has to be something else in the equation, and of course we all know what it is: They're on the stage because they're plugging their latest book, show, recording or whatever.

But do we realize that under the circumstances of getting the stars for only $200 instead of $20,000, the host, and the producers who manipulate the shrieking audiences, can do nothing except extol to the skies the product?

The appearances are *ads*.

The audiences *feast* on the star power while the networks get giant bucks for commercials. In exchange, the shows *automatically tell you* that the new TV series, movie, book, CD, Las Vegas act or whatever is *incredibly good!*

We're being had, and just don't know it.

Critics Aren't Mute, But They're Muted

Critics whether syndicated or hired locally can receive that word to the wise from superiors or editors, "Hey, pal— you're turning off the audience" or the readership, and that others might do a better job. These things have a muting effect. The bottom line, not the expert opinion, governs.

Even the most independent-minded critic appearing on TV has to consider how many stations are buying the show — and be certain these or their audiences aren't offended.

I remember the days when a single newspaper critic of Broadway shows was a czar able to kill with one review. That wasn't right, but today I no longer bother to watch or read any so-called entertainment "criticism" because of economic necessity it's geared to popularity.

The "Plush New Company Sto'"

Nothing has ever so thoroughly enchanted yet encapsulated people like the "plush new company sto'."

From legend and song, we've all heard about the *old* "company sto' which sold grits, salt, and flour in cloth bags for flour-sack dresses—and which loaned money till Friday when the company's slave wages turned out to be less than the amount necessary to cover the store's tab.

The result: "I owe my soul to the company sto'."

The *modern*, disguised company sto' (no longer one company but a group) is deluxe, selling everything including holidays and cruises.

And now you owe for the rest of your life.

In the new system, you're given money several ways: via a job that pays you enough to buy what the companies sell; via loans on credit cards, also for cars and houses.

Then—zip!—all proceeds return to the top because the money's attached by a big rubber band.

To put things another way, we're inside a giant money-vacuuming machine—their vacuum, your earnings.

The Government, which once *bitterly opposed* the sto', now *loves* it, and is *on its side in all matters*.

In fact, the companies have just about bought the type of government they want; therefore, the "company sto'" is far more comprehensive than we believe.

Clutter Blocks Necessary Change

The clutter, commercial encapsulation, and substitution of an end-time mortal realm for the one we should be seeking, are a long way from tending sheep all night on the Canaan hills while watching the stars and contemplating the nature and presence of God.

Cluttering our access to God and diverting our attention prevents or slows the revolutionary changes and empowerments necessary to overcome evil in the end times.

< >

13
INDIVIDUAL EFFORT

Organizations dominate our nation and world, but as our democracy becomes more spiritual, our higher identity under God will make the individual the most important thing once again.

At our founding, individual citizens were widely heard, and there were only a few organizations. Today, one can't be widely heard without credentials from a large organization. This has the effect of eliminating individual opinions and replacing these with organizational opinions delivered by spokespeople.

Can Individuals Frustrated By
Lack Of A Voice In The Modern World
Turn To Media For Help?

Lemme put it this way: media companies are owned by giant conglomerates that may be owned by other conglomerates which make up part of the "group monopolies" comprising the plush new company sto' which is soothing and seducing you even as it "wraps you up," baby.

Try screaming to your local newspaper. It may publish a letter, but it mainly wants local stories and humor.

If you holler to radio talk shows, you may be warmly received as another of the raving lunatics who make great fodder for stirring up comment—and you might get a few minutes of air time. But at the most you'll generally reach only a portion of a highly-sliced-up listenership pie in a regional or local market which would rather be discussing the latest mass suicides.

To get heard at national levels, you have to be a spokesperson for some group's views, not your own. High-ranking people in organizations including the military have retired early to give their own views in books or on the lecture circuit. (Sadly, many have found that once they weren't representing an organization, they had trouble gaining a wide platform.)

Mere citizen status plus solid ideas have no wide platform anymore, and this change is very recent.

Complain To The Government?

Will the Government sound the alarm and make changes? Nah. The Government consists today mainly of people who got into office, and who stay there, chiefly through donations from companies or bigwigs related to corporate or other interests. That's on both sides of the aisle. Some donors give equally.

We got the Government off our backs; however, in its retreat, the corpocracy got *on*.

Government by corporations is here, but still in a relatively benign stage by comparison to its awesome potentials for power.

The Gov't Once Had Antitrust Laws?

Antitrust laws existed to prevent companies from absorbing or destroying their competition, growing gigantic, owning the people... and the Government.

But today's national regulators no longer have the will to control domestic corporations. As for the world scene, nations cannot control the globals even if they want to.

Domestic policy is to allow two biggies to remain (like two soft drink bottlers).

"Global" is one reason given for the lack of anti-monopoly policy. "We have to compete," we're told; and some of the giant companies in other nations are monopolies, even supported by governments. For example, Holland's airline.

In the name of "global competition," we might someday have only one remaining US passenger jet manufacturing company competing with one remaining EU passenger jet manufacturing company.

Wait a minute! That's what we have now!

And we hear open advocacy of doing away with antitrust laws entirely.

Banks Are Consolidating

Remember when banking was mainly local and statewide? Only a few years after regional banking was authorized, firms can now do business coast to coast. Do analysts forecast dozens operating from sea to shining sea? Nope, all recognize that mergers will reduce the total number of big banks to just two or three in time—the "only" banks of any consequence left.

And as for you—you insignificant depositor, you (and I say that with a smile, podnuh)—you're going the way of the "voter."

Already we hear that "tellers" to serve you will disappear, and that there will be a $5 charge if one wants a teller.

When questioned, banks say they don't really want small depositors because they're a nuisance, taking up most of the banks' time and effort, while the money is made with the big accounts.

Local banks will still start up, but with the hope of being bought out for a big price.

Can Giant Food Companies Buy Supermarket Chains?

Consider the consolidation of food companies, and how they now control the market shelves with their major brands —almost all the brands that exist.

Food marketing *is* "shelf space." No more, no less. And the biggies control that limited space.

Do the major food companies feature their names on everything they own? Not if they bought the old "household name" brand for its acceptance, and want to avoid interfering with that recognition. However, in tiny letters on the side, the label states the brand is owned by the big outfit.

Already, small food companies start up and *try* to establish a niche on the shelves mainly with an eye to being acquired by the giants for a handsome stack of common stock certificates.

To break onto the shelves, new companies need massive advertising, so they often have to get a venture capital fund to help them, and thus lose much of their control.

We hear that corporate "bigness" no longer matters.

But what if BigFood Conglomerate starts buying National ShelfSpace Food Markets? And maybe not directly—which might stir up reaction—but through overseas subsidiaries, a little bit here and a little bit there?

Gradually, they can stock two-thirds of each store with their stuff, and charge others seeking shelf space even more money than is now charged. They can crowd out competition, charge you more, give less service and poorer quality.

When We Complain To Gov't About Bigness,
We Quickly Find....

We find the Government on the side of bigness in business. That's a total reversal in only twenty years.

Globals Have Clout

If your nation's government or laws irritate superbusiness, it can—and does—say things like, "Make concessions or we'll move to Mozambique."

Caving in to such threats, the US and others enact special laws, grant favors, pay large sums in inducements, create lower taxation (or no taxation) for periods of time.

Even The NFL

Even NFL franchises inside the US say, "Build us that stadium and rent it to us for next to nothing, and maintain it, and give us the revenue from food and drink sales, and... and...and...*or else we'll move to another city, which has promised us everything we want.*"

And then what will the suffering psyches of your city's population do when they don't have a *ball team* to vicariously identify with?

The bigger organizations grow, the more they get what they want either by shoving governments around or smoothly seducing them.

In all this, the democracy-individual is lessened.

Surely We Can Still Get Around All These Things By Arousing The Mass Voter To Action!

You want to stir up the mass voter? Well, "mass voter" may be an oxymoron. The mass with the greatest amount to lose in all this is the most mute in voting.

Besides, the nominating process for national political office is all in the hands of similar parties, both favoring the present "company sto'." Attempts to warn about organizationalism and boost individuals have no voice.

However, some candidates *offer* to strengthen the individual's hand—screaming about "special interests buying influence" and "the waste of tax dollars." Sadly, most cynically know their campaign-rhetoric proposals won't fly once they're presented to Congress.

How About Starting A Third Party
To Stand Up For The Common Man?

Start a third party? I'm for a dozen parties and coalition governing, because each such party then stands for *distinct things* (in contrast to the positions of the present two parties which are amalgams of all sorts of views homogenized in political balance, watered down, and stirred around).

With multiple parties, the variety of positions usually gets covered by the press.

Despite this, in the US, no third party—much less a fifth or tenth—has been able to gain a permanent footing.

So to whom, or through whom, are you going to complain, folks? And what does this say about democracy?

How About Trying Some Of The
"New World"-Type Systems?
Will They Get You Out— Or In Deeper?

In one "new world" scenario, technology people will continue to invent wonders, and combine with a corporate-type government to have a clean and "efficient" system.

(Shining projections for this sort of thing don't explain how they get rid of the "inefficient.")

Democracy requires that the people know what the hell is going on, and that they are able to control things (or at least keep them within limits).

However, already controlling government, business, the military, transportation, and so on, is technology.

Technology, as it advances further into *technocracy* (government by technology and those who can invent, install, and maintain it), will block democracy's control.

Technological advances will increasingly challenge informed voting, the root of democracy. Already present is a "new illiteracy" (in matters of technology) that could make *effective* voting, and hence control, as obsolete as it was once impractical in an earlier age of illiteracy in *letters*.

The Prophetic Movie "Rollerball" *Gave Us A Great Example Of Corpocracy Combined With Technocracy*

The new world system in *Rollerball* replaced nations and put down the individual after installing "The Corporation" as the *government,* following "the corporate wars."

Steely-eyed John Houseman ran things for the largely-unseen Board.

James Caan, the champion of the brutal world sport, wanted to learn how his rights had suddenly become very limited while he was paying attention to the game. Asking the super-computer that knew everything, he learned all books and history had been revised into authorized edited versions that essentially told him nothing.

The information Caan needed had vanished. He found himself with no information, sources, recourse, or voice.

Houseman lets all know, "Individual effort is futile," as he tries to force Caan, who displays too much of it, to be "retired from the game."

The "individual effort" of *voting* had also become "futile"—having slipped away while voters were absorbed in "the game." Or—apropos of today—other entertainment?

Are elements of *Rollerball* creeping up on us in various ways and forms visible and invisible today? You bet.

We Like Many Of Our Companies, But We Didn't Ask Them To Govern Us

We can't build airplanes in the Wright Brothers' bicycle shop anymore, so we need some big organizations. But we didn't ask them to govern us.

To counter present trends which are gradually usurping democratic governing, individuals need clearer spiritual vision plus vigorous practice of what they find. Groups, organizations, and denominations may assist, but the seeker's effort is the absolute key to a higher democracy right here without changing our existing ordained framework.
So what are we doing about all this?
Well...we're watching "Batman."

Corporate Nations Are Feasible Now

Do we realize there's nothing to keep corporations from setting up *their own nations?*

Companies could set up in sub-Saharan Africa (where the population is leaving due to the creeping desert), or in any sparsely-populated area few want, where today's technology could easily handle the problems of desolateness.
Many weak nations might be willing to sell a chunk of their territory for the right price, especially if an inpouring of capital, water supplies, jobs, or whatever was part of the deal. Or they might just be unable to prevent takeover.

The areas don't have to be big. Monaco is only 368 acres, San Marino twenty-four square miles. If management wanted enough room for a military establishment, sixty-two square miles (the size of Liechtenstein), might do it....

In my novel *Sea Nation* (see bibliography), futuristic oil production platforms put legs down on the Mid-Atlantic Ridge. It's in international waters, and belongs to no one else. This is entirely feasible.

Why submit to a lot of regulations, graft, taxes, customs inspections, lobbying, and ass-kissing of officials in, for example, Ratsassistan, when one can set up one's own nation with the blessings of the well-paid-off seller nation (or its top dogs).

Then, with high-tech weaponry....

Well, with high-tech weaponry, the corporations would not have to keep any promises on which they wished to renege. That ought to appeal to a lot of them.

Mere ultrasonic sound waves could fence off vast desert areas, allow in only those animal herders willing to be the bag-carrying class.

As for mysterious disappearances, who would know? There aren't any birth certificates, I.D. cards or tax numbers in the lower Sahara.

Hell, if a corporation will cut off a thirty-year employee two weeks before his or her pension activates, it's easy to imagine what it would do to undeveloped areas where it had its own press, courts, penal system, police, military, "efficiency squads," and so on.

I think corporate nations—for better or worse—are just around the corner.

New Hope For Individuals In Cyberspace?

The trouble with seeking a new world or escape from the old in cyberspace is that there's no real "realm" there (as so many hope and as some plainly believe), or "new reality" either. Everything depends on whether it's plugged in.

Certainly cyberspace is *immensely useful* for information (a huge electronic library) and for communicating.

Is the growing global internet a type of "communal consciousness"? I'll agree it has aspects of this phenomenon which are little understood, and in that sense it's a sort of "realm." At the least, there's a yearned-for connection with all other people (beyond the long-existing phone system).

Users can "self-publish" in cyberspace on any topic, but will any important numbers of inquirers "hit" the website, absorb much, or change anything in the big, bad world?

Unfortunately, cyberspace spreads rumors, and does this with the great speed of modern equipment. Outrunning the corrective process built into traditional media, this could become a problem in the change-seeking last days.

If a traditional newspaper publishes an incorrect report that stirs up a lot of people, it will usually print clarifications. Calm editorials and explanations appear. Later, syndicated columnists weigh in.

Tabloids may print fabricated stories with no retractions, but people take their features with a grain of salt.

The kingdom of TV is no different. On the one hand is the steadiness and deep background of, say, Jim Lehrer and his panels, or of Sunday opinion shows and network newscasts. And on the other hand, we can watch some pretty low segments in "tabloid" type shows.

What, then, of "cyberspace"?

It's partly a press medium, has a reputation for excellence in education, and also has a dark side.

It has no "old hands" in charge and no valued "credibility" on which its future depends. No political body has yet dared to regulate even its pornography. It can say or depict anything it wants to anyone. It's outside and above most law.

The Possibility Of Sudden (And Even Irresponsible) Changes In World Thought Facilitated By The Net

Consider that unbridled enthusiasm for some "new world" system could with electrifying suddenness sweep the global net, stirring populations to support (even worship) new figures or causes, or to rebel against established ones.

(An example of a sort of communal-mind action was the fall of the Shah of Iran, head of the US-backed third-greatest military power on the globe, whose regime collapsed when the population—acting on some unseen mutual mental signal—just quit on him.)

Long before cyberspace, Mark Twain said a lie gets halfway around the world while the truth is putting on its shoes. This could apply to any wild ideas put on the net.

The net gives us a system for delivering worldwide any information true or false. Orson Welles scared the nation with his "Martians landing" hoax.

There's tinder globally as those with a stake in the status quo are a shrinking percentage while the lean and hungry are growing a billion a decade. The latter may panic (aided by the internet) at the speed with which a few are locking up everything, and the sight of the train leaving the station.

We've all seen how fast an *idea* can shift the fortunes of people, nations, corporations. Computers have changed the world in only fifteen years.

It would be unfortunate if the world's underlying demand for democracy, personal freedom, and a voice were to find irresponsible expression ignited by misinformation, oversimplification, and emotion.

Where there's expectation and hope for change, a leader could arise with a huge following overnight.

Bible and other prophets have predicted the sudden rise of important negative figures and activities in the endtime—things that will appear attractive on the surface, engendering large followings.

Will cyberspace play a role in any of this?

The Bible also tells us God's outreach will be vast. "In the last days, saith God, I will pour out of my Spirit upon all flesh" (Acts 2:16-17).

Drugs?

Some think drugs are a way of escaping systems, walls, pressures. The nurse in *Fort Apache, The Bronx* said they were a "vacation"—that is, until she OD'd.

Marijuana, crack, heroin, meth and new chemical inventions every year are used to dull unknown and known psychological agonies resulting from the end-time double spike and other aspects of this "non rose garden" world.

The user thinks another consciousness is obtained through drugs, and it is—but it's a phenomenon cf his or her own consciousness. It's mere escapism without really going anywhere, and certainly without overcoming.

Double-Death Venues?

Youth and many young adults have slipped into the strange world characterized by mega death type (or double death) entertainment. There are horrifying "virtual reality" and other games in the genre. Posters depict living-death skulls with red, shining eyes, seas of cadavers struggling in dark vapors, and so on.

Popular movies and theme park shows play to the appetite for this sort of thing.

It's the "living death" concept.

That is, the dead are dead in the sense of skulls and corpses, but yet there's *life in them, in this special realm.*

It's a nether world, but it has come to the surface now.

The double spike may be coming down, but this is a way you can join death yet still live, act, be.

It's a giving-in to the end-time spike: glamorizing the death force, and accepting a new, or double depth to so-called death-life or "mortal life."

Everywhere we turn today, death is overemphasized. Yet, Jesus' teachings showed the overcoming of death.

Suicide Enthusiasts
From Ancient Times To Today

Suicide has always been perceived as a "way out." Saul in the Bible fell on his sword to avoid capture. Today's "assisted suicide" is but one evidence of this particular escape hatch. In our bizarre culture, suicides can be so publicized that the figures become celebrities of sorts.

Two factors in suicides are whether oblivion—total zero—is sought, or a *journey*, perhaps to some asteroid.

"Heaven's Gate"—from the beginning—was a journey "outta here." The group didn't like this place, and they stated their reasons. Soon they made plans....

(The Jonestown mass suicide wasn't in either category. The imbibers hadn't been told anything.)

In recent decades, Iran encouraged warriors against Iraq to die in righteous war and thus be granted entry into heaven.

Individual Arab suicide bombers wreaking havoc in the Mideast in modern times consider themselves thereby guaranteed a spot in heaven.

Religious Suicide Even In Early Times

Going back to early times in both Eastern and Western religions, we find self-immolators who burned up their bodies as a means of paying the price, cleansing themselves from sin and the world, and entering heaven. (We hear of modern cases even today.)

Religious suicide may seem a better choice than facing an implacable or unpredictable tough God.

Holy And Other Fire In The Bible

In the Bible, we read that God will destroy the entire earth by fire (II Pet. 3:12).

But the Bible also speaks of "world without end" (Eph. 3:21). Can these two positions be reconciled?

Malachi writes of sweating out our evils much as ore is smelted over fire. That isn't, then, destruction.

"Holy Ghost fire" cleanses our souls and changes our very makeups. That's good stuff causing healing and progress, not annihilation and termination in the typical sense.

This is not to say that the Bible doesn't predict immense upheaval with bad results for many. However, the good God doesn't send evil. The "wrath" is from the "devil" (who, in Revelation 12, is cast from heaven "into the earth," where he exhibits "great wrath, because he knoweth that he hath but a short time").

This devil or "liar" blames God for the horrible acts, deflecting charges (in the traditional manner of the biblical carnal mind) onto another, shifting the true blame from himself by creating false blame against others.

God doesn't kill. Instead, He helps save often worthless butts.

When one calls upon Him as if He were a merciless killer, one may not be open to receive the good results He's always offering, because one is blocking the door to one's own thought.

When you "call upon him in truth," He's "nigh" (Ps. 145:18).

Biblical Ascension's Zero Earthly Remains Vs. Suicide's Remains

In biblical ascension, the body translates in the presence of the higher being, leaving no earthly remains.

This contrasts sharply with thirty-nine corpses from the "Heaven's Gate" mass suicide left behind.

The Next Level

After dying, ordinary people enter a higher state. In the act of passing, many recognize friends who've gone before.

I don't think this is "heaven" in the full sense, but just a state of consciousness above this one. I believe the occupants will find death there until they clear this up in their own thought as they move forward spiritually.

Will Armed Revolution Win For The People, Throw Off The Yoke, And So On?

Some militias here, and revolutionaries worldwide, advocate overthrow of whatever they fancy is causing their problems—while often missing the real problems.

The result of most revolutions throughout history has been to produce a system—or even a chaos—worse than the one they replaced.

After the Czars were overthrown, their replacements formed the most oppressive regime in history. As for small nations, their "coups" usually install "juntas" or the like.

On the other hand, the US, following a genuine spiritual vision, had a successful armed revolution which resulted in great things for itself and the world.

War Upon Others—The "Glory," Etc.

Throughout history, wars of aggression have taken the minds of humans off their problems as they expand into "new fields to conquer...."

Young men join wartime armies on either side in a

heartbeat because there's some *ethos* they perceive in war: some cause, purpose, sense of triumph, glory or whatever. These feelings cause peoples and nations to believe that war will *fulfill,* change, produce the new order they've been looking for.

In no way do I put down the glory of defense of one's own nation if in a genuinely righteous position such as Great Britain's in World War II. Indeed, instances of defense can rise to inspiration on occasion.

It's the glory of aggression that needs to be debunked.

Sherman rightly called most war "hell."

Will billions of people respond to some global "communal consciousness" call to march to war—possibly motivated by anger and envy after comparing their lives to those seen on TV (now that satellite services make many channels available worldwide) and ignited by revolutionaries or hypnotic leaders on the internet?

The Bible speaks of a mystical call to war, gathering the nations and armies to Armageddon.

The Best Way Out Is The Divine "Way"

The "Israel" state of gradually-transformed being is the "generation" that will see the kingdom come, and this progressively advancing state will produce (by stages, not all at once) the divinely-governed individuality that will not be diminished by end-time events and forms, but have "dominion" as the Bible says in Genesis.

The US will continue to lead the worldwide activity.

< >

14

NEW/OLD CIVILIZATION EMERGING

Summarizing The Civilization Now Emerging

The Promised-Land-seeking, Jacob-change civilization has existed from Abraham (circa 1950 B.C.) forward. Early Christianity's profound human changes, healings, and empowerments also came from encounters with the divine.

The questers were often attacked, and never really assimilated. Those who reached the New World found better opportunities. The modern restoration of divine healing and related benefits has produced a broad boom.

Meanwhile, Western Civilization (begun in Greece mainly in the 400s B.C., and later augmented and expanded to the present) became the European and US culture.

The two civilizations, although treated as parts of one entity, were never the same. Today, the spiritualized civilization, now distinct and identifiable, is rising, lifting with it the higher and better elements of the West, while much of Western Civilization is in a downward secular trend.

As The New/Old Civilization Progresses Farther, We Can Expect Several Things

First, Changes In Ourselves

More people than ever will experience healings and all manner of Jacob-to-Israel type changes including instances of protection, guidance, supply, and empowerment as the result of divine encounters. Also, the average individual, who today is being diminished and rendered less and less effective, will become more effective.

Since these things have been the subject of much of this book, I won't recap.

Second, Beneficial Changes In The US

A better democracy is made from better individuals.

Democracy will be greatly strengthened when the average, mass individual (the root unit in a democracy), obtains deeper views of the divine government and sees how these agree with and offer extension to the highest ideals of the US founding.

The US will also benefit when individuals thus enlightened are our officials in place of any who might have narrow concerns not in the best interests of the people.

High-minded elected officials were necessary at the beginning of our democracy-based republic. For example, Washington, when offered a kingship, declined, having a higher vision for America.

However today, dangerously on the increase in the US are persons elected to act in the interests of the people as a whole, who instead serve special constituencies or their own ends.

Without unselfed, even inspired, patrons of the mass, republics can easily become controlled by a few.

God-oriented republics must have unselfed officials.

Someday, individual voters will be so spiritually developed and God-governed that they'll be less dependent on officials and hence closer to a divinely-based democracy.

Earlier in this book we looked at "short" democracy where voters can't control the top of their own government much less the "suprazone" of global commerce and finance which is exercising ever-increasing governmental influence over traditional governing bodies.

The voters in the spiritually-developed US to come will be able to run the nation. They will also handle the overzone supragovernment because the highest "zone" is God and the highest government His divine kingdom (always present here but now coming to our thought).

Thus, "short" democracy will end in the US, and end here before it ends elsewhere.

As America reaquaints itself with its spiritually-ordained nature, hedonism here will begin to precipitate out. The spiritual (which has always been present in our national consciousness), will rise, the other sink—intensifying and battling before losing its footing.

US progress will be obvious to the world, furnishing inspiration and leadership in spiritual matters and practical effects on bodies, lives, and governments, obtainable from encounters with the divine.

The US will lead the world in revelations and results.

Third, The Oppressed Class Worldwide
Will In Time Throw Off Oppression

The oppressed class worldwide will obtain new hope and status through direct relationship with God, eventually (after tribulation and time) overcoming oppression.

The key step in awakening the oppressed of the world to the potentials of divine power will be the end-time waves or "outpouring" of the Holy Spirit "on all flesh" prophesied in Acts and Joel.

The resultant direct worship will start at once to reveal unlimited possibilities for improvement in the human condition and status for even the lowest levels globally.

Democracy in its best forms will be necessary to uninterrupted and speedy, ongoing spiritual progress, lest the heavy boot once again suppress it.

Why is democracy (US democracy in particular) so important to throwing off oppression?

Democracies (or democracy-based republics, which all democracies have been) aid humanity's spiritual progress because freedom of religion, thought, and expression are conducive to divine changes (and vice versa).

Democracies generally *permit* spiritual activity, while empires, old-style autocratic monarchies, dictatorships, religious hierarchies, juntas and the like, often block, target, hunt down, beat up, charge, jail, even murder, proponents.

Are the many newer democracies worldwide conducive to spiritual growth that overturns oppression? Not always, because outer appearances can mask controls by old systems. The words such as parliaments, courts, rights, and voting can sound great, and laws and constitutions be laudable; however, on closer examination, and in practice, constitutional provisions, democratic governing, and the courts and justice systems may be weak, allowing the top to continue to rule and the bottom to still suffer many forms of oppression and exclusion, some harsh.

Where democracies aren't centered on the divine vision but on a material dream—or where "democracy" is mostly rhetoric to pacify the masses while the few continue to run the show, pocket the gains, and own the businesses and land—the people will naturally struggle.

Nonetheless, any form of democracy is better than the top-heavy governments predicted for the end-time.

The Bible predicts end-time persecution of Christians. Some say this is going on today in a more widespread way involving more people than at any time in history.

Fourth, The "City Foursquare" Will Progressively And Someday Totally Replace The Pyramid

The Bible's city with equal sides (Rev. 21:2,16) allows anyone and everyone to be at the top. There are no ever-smaller levels as one goes up, and no bottom with misery, oppression, victimization, or blocked exits.

Mere glimpses of the coming of this new formation has already panicked the pyramid into consolidations toward the one prophesied power.

The "city foursquare" is the form closest to democracy. In sharp contrast, the pyramid is unequal and autocratic.

If allowed to proceed to its ultimate, the pyramid consolidates into a single unit or an amalgam of many interlocking units controlling people. (Whereas the pyramid has shown it can be a handy tool for organizing, that condition exists only where it's controlled by the people, and kept separated and numerous.)

The pyramid, now in a boom stage, is making its move; however, it's already obsolete because it cannot handle the sheer volume of people rising, demanding, and needing access to opportunity and position now that rights are universally proclaimed (and even the remotest hamlets and bottommost strata of life are made aware of possibilities through radios and TVs).

Every time a democracy appears worldwide, it replaces (at least in part) a government which was basically pyramidal. Therefore, is the way is open for the divine system? No, because, as mentioned earlier, the vast global "overzone" of commerce and finance is an ever-increasing pyramid over and above all nations, with their economic existence dependent on playing ball with this super-pyramid "over all"—"uber alles."

Also, again as mentioned earlier, limitations in the newer democracies allow the old power-groups, people, and ways to continue to dominate.

Fifth, We Can Expect Struggles, "666," And Climaxes

The age-old struggles will come to a head. Evil will exercise its full "double" power and (in various climaxes) ultimately so fail as to be placed, its size sharply reduced, in a secondary role to the victorious divine power.

The US will lead in overcoming the climactic "666" and super-pyramid, but not before getting back in touch with its spiritual origins. In the effort, it will have to undergo immense spiritual development in order to survive, but survive, and win, it will.

Those whose names are written in the "book of life" aren't subject to "666" (see Rev. 13: 7-18, particularly v. 8). There will be more people in the US using the "double" power, which involves a degree of awareness of spiritual identity in the "image of God" (and hence written in the "book of life") than elsewhere.

The Sixth Thing We Can Expect Is The Millennium

The "thousand years" that follow the placing of the defeated devil into the pit will witness further spiritual awakening and progress. At the end, the devil will get out of the pit for a final takeover attempt, but will be quickly and permanently terminated, being but a mere shadow of his former self, so to speak. (Rev. 20:2,3,7-10; 21:4.)

Meanwhile, The Search Goes On

Searchers for the Promised Land, obtaining spiritual encounters and human upgrades, have produced a civilization which, through continuing growth in all aspects, will fulfill both the promises of the Bible and the idealism inherent in the US founding.

< >

BIBLIOGRAPHY

Bartleman, Frank *Another Wave Rolls In!* Voice Publications, Northridge (CA), 1970 edn.

Bruce, F.F. *Bible History Atlas.* Crossroad Publishing Co., New York, 1982.

Daiches, David *Moses—The Man And His Vision.* Praeger, New York, 1975.

Eddy, Mary Baker *Science and Health with Key to the Scriptures.* The Christian Science Publishing Society, Boston, 1907, 1934.

Frazer, James G. *The Golden Bough.* Crown Publishers, Inc., New York, 1981 edn. (First published 1890 by MacMillan, London).

Funk, Wilfred *Word Origins.* Bell Publishing Co., New York, 1978.

Gilbert, Martin (1) *Atlas Of American History.* Dorset Press edn., New York, 1984.

Gilbert, Martin (2) *Atlas of Jewish History.* Dorset Press edn., New York, 1984 edn.

Grant, Michael *Atlas Of Ancient History.* Dorset Press edn., New York, 1983.

Hroch, Miroslav and Anna Skybova *Ecclesia Militans—The Inquisition.* Druckerei Fortschritt Erfurt, Edition Leipzig, 1988.

Kinder, Hermann and Werner Hilgemann *The Anchor Atlas Of World History.* Anchor Books Doubleday, New York, 1974 edn.

National Geographic Society (1) *Everyday Life In Bible Times.* Washington, 1967.

National Geographic Society (2) *Great Religions of the World.* Washington, 1978 edn.

National Geographic Society (3) *Greece and Rome, Builders Of Our World.* Washington, 1968.

Roebling, Karl *Sea Nation—Suitcase Supernukes Shake The World.* Dynapress ®, Fern Park, FL ISBN 0-942910-14-1.

Rowland-Entwistle, Theodore *The Illustrated Atlas Of The Bible Lands.* Longman Group Ltd, Harlow (Essex), 1981.

TIME-LIFE (1) *Great Ages of Man—Classical Greece.* New York, 1965.

TIME-LIFE (2) *The Great Ages of Man—Cradle of Civilization.* New York, 1978 edn.

TIME-LIFE (3) *Great Ages of Man—Imperial Rome.* New York, 1965.

Williams, Larry *The Mount Sinai Myth.* Wynwood Press, New York, 1990. (ISBN 0-922066-45-0. Copies obtainable from author: 140 Marine View Drive, Suite 204, Solana Beach, CA 92075.)

Magazines

Archaeology, Boston, MA (author's archive).
Bible Review, Washington, DC (author's archive).
Biblical Archaeology Review, Washington, DC (author's archive).
Christian History. Carol Stream, IL (author's archive).
National Geographic, Washington, DC (author's archive).

Video Tapes

Gilbert, Martin *Jerusalem.* The History Channel, New York, 1996.
(Video tapes, two-volume set.)

"Text Maps"

Selected maps of historical lands with extensive accompanying text, by
National Geographic Society, Washington DC.
Special map showing Pastor Dr. Karl Schott's estimates of wanderings
and new identities of the lost tribes of Israel. Obtainable from *The
Pathfinder,* PO Box 291, Spokane, Washington, 99210.

General Reference

Encyclopedia Britannica (1964 edn.)
Holy Bible - King James Version (KJV). (All Bible quotations in the text
are from this version.)

Our Slogan Is:
DYNAPRESS—IT'S DIFFERENT

Individual, not organizational, thoughts and experiences.
Ideas not personalities are the credentials.
Not written for same old market slots.

The individual is as important to the rebirth and progress of America as to its founding.

The citizen-thinkers who founded this country would likely not be heard today because one must represent giant organizations, and speak through huge media and publishing conglomerates. Organizations are useful but the nation never intended them to crowd out individuals. At the very least today, there should be more seats at the table for citizen thinkers.

Ideas are the credentials at Dynapress, not personalities.

Serious thought can be interesting and engaging; and is essential in a world with so many problems and rapid changes.

Dynapress publishes what needs to be said—not just what fits a market slot. It's different. See our web information on last page.

**Your Comments And Experiences
Are Invited**

Write to:

Dynapress®
Karl Roebling
PO Box 300866
Fern Park FL 32730-0866

(Fern Park is in the Orlando area)

**For Catalog Of Titles
Or To Place Orders**
Write the above address, or
contact our web page at
www.dynapress.com

e-mail: itsdifferent@dynapress.com

FAX: (407) 331-5550